PATRONS.
Field-Marshal SIR DOUGLAS HAIG,
K.T., G.C.V.O., G.C.B.
Field-Marshal LORD FRENCH,
G.C.V.O., G.C.B., K.C.M.G.

BLIGHTY

Offices: 40, FLEET STREET, LONDON, E.C.4.

All profits from this CHRISTMAS NUMBER will be applied to the ordinary weekly issue of "BLIGHTY," which is published exclusively for our sailors and soldiers and sent to them FREE.

MacFARLANE'S GOODWILL.

By GUNNER A. TERBEEGE.

It was very hard to believe but it was a fact.

The morrow was the 25th December. Christmas Day! "Peace on earth, goodwill to all men!" What a mockery those words constituted to the handful of men who occupied the series of shell holes in front of Ypres.

Instead of the village lanes, with their hedgerows lined with clean white snow, there were heaps of sandbags, loose chalk, or cakes of mud. Snow there was none, although it was cold enough for anything. It had rained pitilessly for for the past forty-eight hours, endowing the shell-pocked land with the clinging tenacity of an octopus. One associated Christmas Eve with church-bells and carol singing, but their places were taken by the chimes of 4.2's and the musical "zip-zip" produced by energetic machine-gunners.

On one of the rough fire-steps were a couple of Highlanders. Their rifles rested upon the parapet over which they gazed from time to time. Water ran off their caps, noses and ears, while their boots seemed to ooze with moisture.

The one was a big brawny fellow of the morose type, but his companion was small of stature and his looks betrayed joviality.

"Well, Mac, what be ye thinkin' aboot?"

The tall Scot grunted. "Nowt."

"Noo, Mac, dinna fash yersen. To-morrow is Christmas, laddie. Jist mind 'on it. Bells ringin', plenty o' beer, heaps wee lassies, lots o' dancin', roarin' fire——"

"Hould yer whist, will ye, Sandy Waterson. Dinna drive a feller mad."

"Noo, noo, ye cross old Scotchman. Bide a wee while. Anither half-'oor and we'll be relieved. Then the dug-out and rum, Mac, real rum. Rum that maketh glad the heart o' men."

"Aye, I ken weel, Sandy, but I'd like to ha' a go at yon blokes to-night. Tae think we suffer a' this just acause them sausage eaters o'er yon."

He wiped the wet off his bayonet affectionately.

"MacFarlane, ye blood-thirsty Hielander. De ye ken what the parson in the kirk is preaching the noo. 'Peace on earth, goodwill to a' men.'"

"I ken weel enough. If I had my way

Fastidious Seaman (crossing muddy street): "WHY DON'T THEY SWAB THEIR BLOOMING DECKS SOMETIMES?"
Chas. Grave.

to-nicht they would git peace—a piece of this."

Their conversation was interrupted by the sound of footsteps approaching. Waterson, being nearest, challenged quietly. A password was quickly given and the new-comer turned out to be their platoon officer.

"That you, Waterson and MacFarlane?"

"Yis, sir."

"Good! Well, I want a couple of volunteers to go over on a patrol to-night. The heads suspect a sap is being run out opposite and we have to find out and report. Want the job?"

MacFarlane was all eagerness. He didn't give his pal a chance to reply.

"Yis, sir, what time?"

"Say, in five minutes."

"Right, sir."

MacFarlane hugged his friend with joy.

"He' a rale sport, is wee McGregor." He turned to his rifle and bayonet. "If ye dinna bag a Jerry to-nicht, a'll sell ye."

Five minutes later a cold, wet, but very enthusiastic party of three crept through the barbed wire. MacFarlane took the right, his officer the centre, and Waterson the left.

The big Highlander was the first to give the arranged signal. In front of him was a shallow trench. He crawled noiselessly towards this and found it occupied by a German. The latter was apparently guarding the sap for he held a rifle. Mac's eyes glinted with unholy joy. What a chance! He approached within striking distance and poised his rifle to make the fateful bayonet thrust when a Verey light went up.

He paused in his triumph, for the light revealed one of the most depressed of human beings. Even by the illumination of the star shell the kiltie could see how blue were the features of the German.

"Puir wee divil!" He slung his rifle and tugged at the cork of his water-bottle.

Here, Fritzy, take a nip of this."

He supported the form of his sworn enemy and poured rum through the closed lips.

He was doing this when his companions came up. Between them they got the reviving figure into their own lines.

After he had gone Waterson turned to the solemn-looking MacFarlane.

"Weel, Mac, how many Jerrys did ye k——. Why, mon, weer's ye bayonit?"

"Here." The tall Highlander pointed to his scabbard.

"But why, Mac? Ye——"

"It's Christmas."

THE ARMY TOUCH.

By "GUNNER."

We had been exceptionally lucky in procuring "The Gables" for our Convalescent Hospital. At least we thought so when we first approached the building, but closer inspection of the interior had caused us to alter our opinions. Still it had its advantages over some of the barns we had transformed, by the saving grace of umpteen drums of creosol, into a resting place where one might convalesce. The main drawback was the chimney.

This was just an ordinary structure really, but it had been trained badly in its earlier days. It was everlastingly chocked. Perhaps it suffered from perennial abscess in the throat, but anyway, its M.O., the cook, could never prescribe a clearing remedy. It also added to its disagreeableness by suffering generally just in the middle of cooking dinner.

Our C.O. is not a bad sort—as far as his category goes, but he fiercely objected to having a succession of black puddings. How was he to know that one was intended for rice and another for something else, for they were all disguised in a perpetual cover of outer darkness.

Still something had to be done, so I boldly (outwardly, of course) marched into the O.R. to see the B.S.M.

"Whatsermarrer?" was his amiable greeting.

"It's—it's the chimney, sir, it's stuck up."

"Well, get it unstuck."

"Yes, sir." I turned, but, hardly grasping what process would have to be adopted before his most valuable suggestion could be carried out, I ventured to ask to be enlightened.

"Dash it, man," he thundered, "do you want me to do the job myself, or what?" One should always laugh at these awfully witty bursts of humour on the part of S.M.'s. "Fetch the sweep and ask him his price for the job."

"Yes, sir." I dashed out, feeling as large as a diminutive threepenny bit. Then Mr. Smith, the sweep, arrived.

He was a dark horse, metaphorically and literally speaking. When I entered the room I thought he had at least been up the blocked fissure, so black did he look; but no, he was just surveying things.

After performing all those weird antics known only to sweeps, he informed us it would cost 15s. to put our old flu on its legs once more.

The price was condemned by those higher up. The cook assured me it would cost that for beer alone to drink after, if he had taken the job on. So "Signals" got busy, and in due course the following words were being slung about all over the place:

"—TH ARMY, A.A.A.
SEND SWEEP TO-DAY, A.A.A.
URGENT, A.A.A.
—ND, R.A.M.C."

The incinerator squad had just fallen in the next morning when another black figure enters our luminous portals. It was the army sweep, one O.R. After he had unshipped his yards of piping, some of which, naturally, became imbued with a burning desire to peer through the C.O.'s window, he began to negotiate the fateful chimney.

I followed his progress until a pound of soot disarranged the parting of my hair, when I was content to depend upon the verbatim reports of others. All went well until five minutes had elapsed. Then we heard frantic cries from somewhere near the roof. Someone translated his S.O.S. to mean that he was stuck, unable to move, and would someone kindly remove him. Of course, being in the army, he hardly put it like that, but that was how I transmitted it to the S.M.

"Find out what Smith will get him out for."

"Yes, sir." I flew down to the local nigger merchant and explained my urgent business. He was independent.

"Looke 'ere, mister. Yon bloke (our C.O., I presume he meant, how I admired the man's bravado) wouldn't have me. Too dear. Can't give an 'onest chap a livin'."

I assured him of the entire coincidence of my views with his own, and after a little while he came round.

"Well, seein' as 'ow it's a feller bein' in distress, I'll do it fur the same price, fifteen bob."

I slapped him on the back, praising his great sense of duty. Incidentally I couldn't have faced our S.M. without him, so I dragged him up to our show again. Surely this would be the end of our chimney trouble. It was not to be. The S.M. loomed in the landscape.

"Well, Jones, did you get him?"

"Yes, sir."

"What price is he doing it for?"

"Fifteen shillings, sir."

"What? Has that amount been sanctioned?"

"I don't know, sir."

"Don't know, and this man is being allowed to carry on without H.Q.'s confirmation of the price. Do you want to ruin the country and lose the war?"

I meekly opined that nothing was further from my thoughts, but—but Sweep No. 2 was still stuck up the chimney.

"Tell him to wait, then," he shrieked. "When will you learn the correct army way of dealing with these vital matters."

I gave up such a world-wide problem. "Signals" got busy once more as follows:

"—TH ARMY.
Army sweep stuck in chimney, A.A.A. Local man's price fifteen shillings for removing same, A.A.A. Please advise necessary action.
—ND, R.A.M.C."

Never shall I forget the horrible suspense—either my own or that of the sticky sweep—while "Signals" did their best. Cook very optimistically sent word up the chimney that if he, the flu merchant, was not down by the day after to-morrow a tin of Maconachies or bully beef would be dropped down the chimney pot.

At last the reply came, and we eagerly scanned the contents which were most fulsome.

"—ND, R.A.M.C.
You are authorised to remove the sweep at all costs.
—TH ARMY."

Thus ended a black tragedy.

BILL'S FAREWELL.

"Git away wif yer, I'm orf."

"But, Bill, how can I live wifout yer?"

"Garn! Git art of it, sloppy. I've got ter go an' fight."

"But supposin' ——"

"Supposin' nuthin'. Don't 'ang rahnd ma neck. I want that fer me pack, an it'll come in 'andy when the 'Uns are snipin'."

"You might give me a kiss afor yer go."

"Kiss be 'anged! I don't know what you wimmen warnt. 'Ere's a grateful Govment gives yer seperation allowance, twelve-a-tanner a week, all ter yerself, an does a poor chap out a half his bob a day. And then yer 'ang rarnd when he's got ter go, as if yer just got spliced. I should a fort yer'ed bin glad to pick up the splosh an' say nuthin'."

Pte. J. ALLEN.

BRINGING HOME THE XMAS GOOSE. *Poy.*

Rude Boy: "HELLO, MUNITIONS!" — Hutton Mitchell.

"I SUPPOSE YOU HAVE MANY TRIALS, MY GOOD MAN?"
"YES, LIDY, BUT IT'S THE CONVICTIONS WOT ANNOYS ME." — Hutton Mitchell.

THE "SOLDIER MAN" IN THE SOUDAN.

By "YEO" (Author of "Soldier Men").

[SCENE: A large thatched mud hut, very light and airy, in the Acholi district. At a table in the middle the Commandant in a helmet and plume, shirt, shorts, and gaiters; on one side a clerk (Egyptian) in a pink tie and white flannel trousers; three or four black soldier policemen, very smart in uniform. The plaintiff—also a soldier, and also very smart; the defendant and the defendant's brother and sister all absolutely as God made them, and looking rather lost without their spears, which they had been obliged to leave in the cloak-room. Behind a few witnesses, also absolutely stark, and two or three headmen in tarboushes and ivory bracelets.]

THE CASE.

A soldier had complained that someone had stolen his sister. Accordingly, a "paper" was sent to collect the sister and the thief and the thief's wife and the thief's chief, and all and sundry. After about four days they had duly appeared, and all trailed into the office.

Note: The Acholi dialect is so limited that, for instance, the same word stands for brother, sister and cousin.

Then the case begins.
COMMANDANT (to the soldier): "Is this girl your sister?"
"Yes."
Then to the thief:
"Is this girl that soldier's sister?"
This question is duly posted to the thief through the four interpreters (necessary owing to the various local dialects), and in course of time the answer gets back to the Commandant.
"No, she's my wife's sister."
The Commandant (puzzled—to the soldier):
"What's your father's name?"
"Oleng."
"What's this girl's father's name?"
"Oquet."
"Then your father and her father arn't the same?"
"No."
"Is her mother one with your mother?"
"No."
"Then how is she your sister?"
"She's my sister."
A dead wall seems to have been struck!
Then a fresh start is made.
(To the thief): "What's your wife's father's name?"
"Quong."
"Oh! And the girl's father's name is Oquet?"
"Yes."
"Oh! What's your wife's mother's name?"
"Amayu."
"Oh! What's the girl's mother's name?"
"Amayu."
"Oh! Are the girl's mother and your wife's mother one?"
"No."
"Oh!"
Another dead wall.
Then to the soldier again: "Is this girl your father's brother's daughter?"
"Yes."
"Oh! What was your father's brother's name?"
"Oqueqa."
"Oh! And the girl's father's name was Oquet. Are they the same?"
"No."
Then follows a long chat from the soldier which finally gets through to the Commandant via a very excited interpreter, "that the soldier's father's brother married a man from the tribe of the thief, and their son was——"
Commandant: "Wait a minute. Do you mean the soldier's father's brother married a woman, or that the soldier's father's sister married a man?"
Nobody seems to know, so it is posted through to the soldier.
The answer comes back (amid tense excitement): "He says the soldier's father's sister married a woman."
Commandant: "Oh, ask him if his father's brother was a male brother or a female brother?"
"He says a female brother."
And so it goes on for perhaps an hour, till at last the Commandant gets the hang of the case, and starts to state the relationship as he understands it. Breathless excitement in everyone.

Major (to Pte. Murphy flourishing both brushes): "WHAT'S THE HURRY, MY MAN?"
Pte. Murphy: "SURE, SORR, THERE'S ONLY A DHROP OF PAINT LEFT, AN' I WANT THE RAILING DONE BEFORE IT RUNS OUT."

Gnr. R. C. MacPhail, R.G.A.

"GIVE US ANOTHER WOODBINE, BILL, OR I'LL LEAVE YOU TO IT!"
Gnr. O. L. Bullock, Nell Lane Hospital, West Didsbury.

Commandant: "This soldier's father's female brother married a man from the tribe of that man? Tamam (that right)?"

"Aywah," with great satisfaction and eagerness from everybody. (By the way, "Yes" ought always to be a two-syllabled word.)

"They had a son named Oquet?"

"Aywah." Frightful excitement. The strain is almost intolerable now.

"Oquet's daughter was the girl here? Tamam?"

"Aywah." The excitement is reaching a climax.

"The man the soldier's father's female brother married had a female sister who was the mother of that other man's wife. Tamam?"

"Aywah." Great satisfaction all round. General sense of awful strain relaxed.

Everyone much relieved. His "Side" (Sudanese expression of reverence), the Commandant, has understood it all. Everyone (metaphorically) sits back in their chairs, and push back their hats (those of them who have any), and take a breather. Then to it again, to decide who is entitled to the girl—who, by the way, is only about five years old, and takes no interest in the proceedings whatever, being apparently fascinated by the clerk's pink tie!

But here the Court rises for refreshment.

* * * *

Apart from his judicial function a British officer in the Soudan is really more in the position of a feudal over-lord than of a company commander. The men, of course, bring all their wives and children with them, and the company becomes their home. They have no rations, and grow their own corn and keep their own cattle. They feed themselves entirely. The company is their village, and the officer is their headman. He has to build their houses, arrange their drainage system, allot ground for their crops, settle their disputes, and look after them when they are ill. The whole population from which the men are drawn are, of course, complete savages, and the result is the whole battalion has to be run on purely personal lines. For instance, when the recruits take the oath, which they swear on a bayonet, after the prescribed words they frequently add something on their own, such as: "Now I have left my village and my people, and the Commandant is my father."

The "Government" means nothing much to them. They believe the white man's home is Khartoum; they firmly believe their pay comes out of the officer's pocket; they look on the officer simply as a great chief who wants an army, and their loyalty is solely to him personally. They are delightful fellows, very honest and manly and straightforward, ridiculously loyal and staunch, always cheerful and bright, and as keen as mustard. These Acholi are not in the least like the ordinary African. They are a small people, and are very slender and graceful. Their faces are not a bit negroid. Neither are they in the least Arab or Oriental. The real negro face is an exception. Of course, they are as black as your hat, but if you changed the colour of their skins their features would mostly pass as English.

They have delicate, clear-cut features, firm, clean chins, straight noses, with frequently good bridges, and no trace of splayed nostrils, often thin lips and upright foreheads—and all of them have the most winning and delightful smile—not in the least the negro's grin, but a real friendly, open, humorous smile. The cases which come before the officer in the orderly room show how he is regarded, and illustrate how justice is carried out. Here is an instance. A soldier had married a wife just before he joined the army, and paid fifteen sheep for her. After he had been in the regiment a fortnight he sent for her, and she arrived with her father.

Scene: An orderly room. The soldier very smart and stiff in uniform (if only it was not known that three weeks before he had been absolutely stark!), the wife standing behind, rather over-dressed in beads, the father in his Sunday best, consisting of two ivory bracelets and a bit of leopard skin.

The father: "I paid five sheep to the local magician to cast a spell so that my daughter should have a large family. I say that the soldier should pay for those sheep."

Obviously a case of extortion. The wife had been sold for fifteen sheep when the soldier was a civilian, and now that he had enlisted, and was drawing 10s. a month, and was generally the deuce of a nut, the father thought he had better try and extract five more sheep.

Case dismissed; much to the delight of the soldiery.

[NOTE.—After writing "Soldier Men." "Yeo" was transferred from the Bucks Hussars, with which he had served in Gallipoli and in the Senussi campaign, to the Egyptian Army, with the rank of Bimbashi (major), and appointed to a post in the Lower Sudan, where his duties were partly military and partly administrative and judicial. Hence the local colour in the above sketch.—EDITOR.]

ELISE.

There's a sleepy little village just within the French frontier,
   And a little ruined church beneath the trees;
A row of wooden crosses tells the story of our losses,
   And on one you'll read a woman's name "Elise."
In that camp so white and silent, with the martial dead around,
   How is it she has won a place with these?
The curé tells the story, and on France's roll of glory
   No name shines out more brightly than "Elise."

Ere the War Lord's mad ambition had plunged the world in strife
   A simple village maiden could be seen,
With her winsome ways and graces and the prettiest of faces
   She ruled the little commune like a queen.
One day there came a stranger, he was handsome, young and rich,
   He spent his gold with large and lordly ease;
He paid her his addresses, and with presents and caresses,
   Won the loving, trusting heart of our "Elise."

Alas! the story ended, as such stories sometimes do,
   The stranger went away to whence he came;
His promises were broken, no good-byes were spoken,
   He left the girl to solitude and shame.
The curé stoops and places a wreath of woodland flowers
   On the grass that whispers softly in the breeze—
"Oh, forgive our wilful blindness, those that might have shown her kindness
   Were the first to cast a stone at poor Elise."

Came the day when distant cannon thundered out the word of war,
   And the ghastly mills of death began to grind,
When the Uhlan lances shone, and the Prussian horde swept on,
   A trail of burning villages behind.
It was "Food for men and horses!" Brutal soldiers in our homes,
   Sobbing, weeping women on their knees.
Too stunned to seek assistance, too weak to show resistance,
   There was no one gave a thought to poor "Elise."

On the Mairie door one morning a proclamation told
   The body of a soldier had been found,
If no one made confession, to teach the French a lesson,
   The village would be levelled to the ground.
They knew the murdered soldier was the victim of a brawl,
   But what justice could be found in curs like these?
With the danger growing graver, an unexpected saviour
   Came forward, in the person of "Elise."

Forgotten were the insults and the slights she had received,
   Forgotten were the looks of scorn and hate;
One single impulse filled her, and the daring of it thrilled her,
   To save the little village from its fate.
She sought the Hun commander, and her little heart beat fast,
   His savage anger seeking to appease,
With a countenance unaltered, and a voice that never faltered,
   "It was I that killed your soldier," said Elise.

She was shot next morn at sunrise, and they laid her down to rest,
   Our heroine, so noble and so brave.
There she's gently sleeping, while sons of France are keeping
   A deathless guard of honour round her grave.
In the solemn hush of evening, when the sunset's dying rays
   Makes a lane of gold between the watching trees;
It lays a tender finger, seeming lovingly to linger
   On the little mound that shelters our "Elise."

* * * * * *

There's a sleepy little village just within the French frontier,
   And a little ruined church beneath the trees.
The curé tells the story, and on France's roll of glory
   No name is loved more deeply than "Elise."

          Sergt. G. E. ATTWOOD.

THE JORDAN HIGHLANDERS.

"PUT DOWN YOUR HAND, IKEY, PUT DOWN YOUR HAND!—IT'S YOUR DIAMOND THAT'S ATTRACTING THE FIRE!"
          Pte. R. Inward, 2/19th London Regt.

ALL FOR "U."

Signalman H. W. Moller, H.M.S. Menace.

Orderly (aside to Medical Officer who is recalling to patient yesterday's advice that he has only three years to live if he does not give up smoking): "EXCUSE ME, SIR, THAT WAS T. JONES—THIS IS HIS BROTHER JIM—HE'S ONLY GOT A BRUISED HEEL."

L/Cpl. J. Tait, H.M.A.T., Panama.

UP A TREE.

By GEORGE WAIGHT.

If Jimmy had not stopped his motor bike to light his pipe, this story would probably never have been written.

However, he did stop it, and thus it happened that he was able to hear the call which sounded from somewhere close by.

"Help!" the voice called, and Jimmy at once was eager to become a helper, because, for one thing, Jimmy always made a hobby of helping people in distress, and, secondly, the voice gave promise of something fair and feminine, a combination which few men, and certainly never Jimmy, have found it possible to resist.

"Help!" the voice called again, and Jimmy, all anxiety to help, looked round in perplexity to discover where the knight errantry was to begin. At present Jimmy could see nothing but trees, and somehow the trees hardly seemed to fill the bill.

"I'm up here," cried the voice, so Jimmy looked up and scanned the branches of the trees, but in the fading light could still see nothing.

"My ladder has fallen down," the voice continued, just at the moment when Jimmy made acquaintance with the ladder by the simple process of falling over it.

After that he became a veritable sleuth. The ladder was in such a position that it could only have fallen from one of two trees, and he set himself to study the branches of these two in the hope to discover the unusual fauna that was apparently lurking therein.

"Surely you can see me now," a voice grumbled.

"I wish I could," said Jimmy, peering up one tree. Are you up this one?"

"No, of course, I'm not," said the voice somewhere behind him.

Jimmy swung round and gazed upwards at the other tree.

"Wave your arms about," Jimmy requested.

"If I do I shall fall," replied the voice.

"I've got you," he shouted all at once.

"I wish you had," the girl complained.

"I mean," Jimmy corrected himself carefully, "I can see you. Now to business."

After some difficulty he got the ladder fixed against the tree.

"Can you reach it?" he called up.

For answer the girl scrambled quickly down the ladder and stood beside him.

"Splendid," said Jimmy. "May I ask if you make a hobby of living up trees?"

"More or less," said the girl. "I work in this plantation."

"I've seen you often," Jimmy admitted, "as I've passed on my bike."

"I know," said the girl, "I've seen you, too. Well, this afternoon I had to go up this tree to cut off a branch, and while I was up some wretched monkey of a boy pulled the ladder away as a joke. I was sitting on a bough at the time, where I've been ever since. That was about an hour ago."

"Good heavens!" Jimmy exclaimed, "you might have stayed there all night if I hadn't passed."

"I know," said the girl. "But I felt sure you'd pass. You always do about this time."

"I ride over to get the letters," Jimmy explained.

"All I was afraid of," the girl continued, "was that the noise of your bike would prevent you hearing me."

"Lucky I stopped," he commented. "Now, what about home? It's three miles away and it's lighting-up time, and I haven't a lamp. We shall have to get a move on. Hop up."

"How do you know where I live?" she demanded, at the same time climbing on to the carrier.

"I've seen you, of course," said Jimmy, starting up the bike, "but I know a lot more than that. You live at Dean Croft with your aunt, and your name is Janet Fife, and ——"

"How ever do you know all that?" the girl demanded.

"Tactful enquiries," replied Jimmy modestly. "The only thing I didn't know happened to be what I wanted to know most."

"And that?" the girl asked.

"You," replied Jimmy laconically.

"Me?" the girl repeated in amazement. "Well, any way, surely there wasn't much difficulty about that."

"Wasn't there," said Jimmy gloomily; "I couldn't find anyone who knew you. I once nearly stopped my bike and spoke to you."

"Why didn't you, then?" this amazing girl enquired.

Jimmy stood open-mouthed.

"You don't imagine, do you," she continued, "that there's too much fun for me either, living with an old aunt, who is horrified every time she sees me wearing my working breeches (and she indicated with a smile a very dainty pair of green plush bifurcated garments); there's not a jolly soul for me to know here. When I've seen you pass, I'd often have stopped you—made you talk to me, if I'd had the courage—so there!"

Jimmy became embarrassed.

"Heavens!" he exclaimed piously, "to think I've been a fortnight down here wasting my time when I might ——" he broke off hastily. "Never mind," he added, "I've got another week before I return to duty, and I rather fancy ——" but the rest of the sentence was lost in the roar of the engine as Jimmy stopped the bike before the maiden's gate.

"At what time shall I fetch you to take you to work to-morrow?" Jimmy demanded brazenly.

The girl looked a moment at him and then laughed.

"Half-past four," she said.

"Right-ho," said Jimmy unperturbed, "I'll be there."

"Oh, look," Janet exclaimed suddenly, "there's the little wretch that pulled the ladder away.

Jimmy looked.

"Oh, is it?" he said grimly. I'll deal with him. He's the boy that lives in the house where I've taken rooms."

* * * *

Jimmy did deal with him. To be exact, he gave him half-a-crown. That's simple enough. But the point is this, that the lad got altogether five shillings. Now, what I want to know is, where and why did he get the other half-crown?

Lieut. G. WAIGHT.

"HELLO, SANTA!"
Sgt. Will Neil, 10th Black Watch.

THE LAMP DIVINE.

When the sap flowed full and strong, O son o' mine,
I alighted me a lamp—the Lamp Divine—
With a taper, from the altar set on high,
Where the votive lights of pure love never die.

Yet, O son o' mine, all's dark about me now,
As the closing shadows creep around my brow;
For the Lamp Divine just flickered out and died,
And its wraith but hovers near me to deride.

In the temple of my love broods blackest night—
And mine own the hand that blotted out the light.
So, heed then folly's dirge, O son o' mine;
Since it's lighted, keep alight the Lamp Divine.

HARRY BAXTER.

THEIR DUTY—*Your Privilege*

THOUSANDS of Employers are naturally exercised on the subject of additional provision for the dependents of those of their Employees who, on Active Service, may lose their lives—from Ordinary Causes, from Accident, in Action, or from Wounds, &c.

The usual conditions of War preclude protection under ordinary forms of Insurance, yet the need for some form of cover is obvious.

The State very properly provides pensions upon a fixed schedule, but employers recognise that such pensions must frequently be disproportionate to the normal circumstances of the dependents of their employees.

In America the State provides a certain pension, but has in contemplation allowing the individual to apply a certain proportion of his pay in the form of an Insurance Premium to enable him to some extent to rate up the amount his family would receive in the event of death. There is no similar scheme existing at present in this country, but certain adjustments are rendered possible to the individual under

THE WAR LIFE POLICY

OF THE
Eagle & British Dominions Insurance Co.

Under this Policy a sum may be provided for, say,

WIFE, PARENTS, SISTERS OR BROTHERS, EDUCATION OF CHILDREN, DAUGHTER'S FUTURE, BOY'S START IN LIFE, FAMILY AND BUSINESS LIABILITIES.

Minimum Premium.	Maximum Premium.	Maximum Benefit.
£1	£20	£2,000

Varying Benefits based upon most equitable and generous lines according to the Risks to which the Insured Life is exposed.

Trustees for the Fund:
FIELD-MARSHAL VISCOUNT FRENCH,
G.C.B., O.M., G.C.V.O., K.C.M.G.
and
ADMIRAL OF THE FLEET, SIR WILLIAM HENRY MAY,
G.C.B., G.C.V.O.

WRITE TO-DAY (mentioning "War Life Policy") FOR FULL SCALE OF RATES, PROPOSAL FORMS, DETAILS OF RISKS AND INFORMATION AS TO DIVISION OF SURPLUS FUND.

The EAGLE and BRITISH DOMINIONS Insurance Company, Limited.

Life Dept.: **52, THREADNEEDLE ST., E.C. 2.**

Head Office:
British Dominions House, Royal Exchange Avenue, London, E.C. 3.

West End Office: **79, PALL MALL, LONDON, S.W. 1.**

Branches throughout the United Kingdom.

ASSETS EXCEED £5,000,000

APPLICATIONS FOR AGENCIES INVITED.

"SEA PIE"

CHRISTMAS NUMBER.

On Sale Saturday, December 8th.

Price 1/- nett.

Humorous Pictures, Poetry, and Prose, contributed by Frank Brangwyn, H. M. Bateman, Chas. Pears, Dudley Buxton, Bert Thomas, Bertram Prance, Smithson Broadhead, Chas. Graves, Cecil King, Stan Terry, Barribal, Norman Wilkinson, Lander, Hutton Mitchell, Anson Dyer, Geo. Dixon, "Rip," Geo. R. Sims, Bartimeus, Arnold Golsworthy, Cecil Whitehead, Nigel Oliphant, A. St. John Adcock, Keble Howard, Chas. Proctor, A. M. Gordon, Charlotte Mansfield, "The Kernel," Catherine Mais, Lt.-Com. McGill, Capt. Ronald Hopwood, Geo. Edgar, "Poy," and a host of other celebrities.

Every person interested in the Navy should get a copy.

On Sale at all Bookstalls and Newsagents.

40, Fleet Street, London, E.C. 4.

Chicks: "LOOK, MA! BROTHER EGBERT'S SWANKING HE'S A WATER-PLANE!"

Ricardo Brook.

Fish Coster (to member of Chinese Labour Corps): "NAW THEN, RAJAH, 'OW ABAHT AN 'ADDICK FOR THE 'AREM?"

Lt. E. W. Jacot.

NINETTE.

By CHARLES L. WARR,
Author of "The Unseen Host," "Echoes of Flanders," &c.

It was all so very sad, and this old world is sad enough just now in all conscience. But somehow I should like to tell you about Ninette—poor little Ninette. For she was a good sort. She wasn't an aristocrat like the heroines of most stories; she was only the keeper-proprietrix—if you like—of a little pub in Raminghelst; but she was as lovely as the dawn. And beneath the bunch of tricoloured ribbon which she always wore on her left breast there beat as true and courageous a heart as could be found in the Allied line from Ostend to the Vosges. I'm absolutely no use at describing the charms of the fair sex, and, therefore, I'm afraid I can't give you much idea of Ninette—but she had such glorious black hair, clouds of it, in which you saw waves of shifting colour; and her eyes were clear blue like the summer skies of Italy—but sometimes they had strange mists in them, suggestive of the incommunicable things of the soul. Her teeth and her lips were so perfect—they really were. She was just sweet, was Ninette.

Heavens! that estaminet of hers was a godsend to the troops which came back to reserve in Raminghelst. The street in which it stood was almost pounded to bits, and the estaminet was now transferred to what had once been its wine cellar—sand-bagged and bolstered up with logs and earth and wire-netting. And here Ninette presided behind an improvised bar, and dispensed coffee and omelettes, the contents of multifarious bottles, and many a dainty little dish cooked cunningly by herself upon a rather dilapidated stove; and also flirted occasionally with the more attractive of her martial patrons—but only occasionally, and very discreetly, for she was engaged to Jules Cliquot: and there was no one on earth like Jules. She loved him with all the passionate love of her great French heart—and how true and constant a love that is, only those people know who can see through the popular misrepresentations of sixpenny novelettes.

Ninette was an orphan without one living soul in this wide earth to care a sou whether she sank or swam, or cried or smiled, or lived or died. And Jules was her all; and with that all she was well satisfied. She found a lot to be thankful for in that dirty, grimy cellar of hers; for she knew that the greatest things in life are what appear to be our smallest mercies. Which is a lesson that we of the twentieth century are slow to learn—we who find that all is vanity before we leave our twenties. Ninette had much to be grateful for, so she thought in her simplicity; and daily before her little Calvary, set in a niche in the wall, she naïvely thanked the good God that He had made her so pretty, and that men wanted to kiss her and make love to her—although she let no one kiss her, no one but Jules: and also, that Jules was in the trenches before Raminghelst, when he might have been so far away. Oh, yes, there was a lot to thank the good God for; for she was making money . . . money for that home with Jules, which shone through the blood-red mists of war as the lodestar of her life.

She was about the only girl left in Raminghelst—very probably the only one. She had been asked to leave, cajoled to leave, ordered to leave; but she had defied the authorities. And a pretty face makes defiance easy, so Ninette stayed. As long as Jules could stick to his post, so long would she. Mon Dieu, was she not betrothed to a soldier of France?

The months rolled past, and Jules' regiment left for another part of the line. It was a cruel blow to Ninette, but she kept on smiling, and attended to her estaminet, became a trifle more serious, flirted even more occasionally. And daily and nightly, and whenever she could, she prayed by the little Calvary to Mary the Friend of women, that she would intercede with the good God to bring Jules back to Raminghelst; and ten days before the Christmas of 1915, the regiment came back, and Jules with it.

It was then that Ninette made her wonderful plan. It cost her a lot, too; for she had to seek for fellow-conspirators among the men of Jules' company; and when she had chosen them, and taken them into her confidence, they would only help in exchange for a kiss.

She gave it after due consideration, but gave it with a bad grace. She would tell Jules, however, and when he knew all, he would understand and laugh—how he would laugh!

On Christmas Eve the plan was carried to execution, and she paid a secret visit to Jules in the trenches. For she had a romantic little heart, a rare quality in these days, and she wanted to be with Jules at the hour of midnight; that, where he faced the enemy in the peril and squalor of the trenches, there she might listen with him for the

Sylvia (sympathetically): "AND HOW WERE YOU WOUNDED?"
Tommy: "I WAS HIT BY A HIGH EXPLOSIVE."
Sylvia: "GOOD GRACIOUS, HOWEVER COULD THAT HAPPEN? YOU'RE NOT IN THE LEAST TALL."

"*Chalky.*"

songs of the holy angels. Arrayed in a borrowed uniform, her abettors smuggled her into a ration party; and, in the darkness of the night, she plodded up a cobbled, shell-torn road, lined with tall, spectre-like poplars, swaying and swishing eerily in the gloom. Over three fields they wandered, knee deep in mud, then into a winding communicating trench, over whose parapets the bullets began to whine and ping, and ever and anon the party stopped to crouch in the swelling ooze, while star-shells illumined the blackness with a weird white glow. Ninette felt a queer sinking and emptiness in her heart, but she set her teeth and thought of Jules, and crept forward with the rest. At last the journey was accomplished, and Ninette's companions had her safely in the trench; and there, in the secrecy of a traverse, screened from every enquiring eye, Ninette found herself in the arms of her lover.

But Ninette was not to hear the songs of the angels—not in that trench, at any rate. For at ten o'clock the Bosche got the wind up, and a tornado of shells began to batter down between the trench and the support line. For a quarter of an hour the cataract of bursting, screaming metal continued. Then the guns lifted and the range altered. Immediately the tempest burst on the front line trenches, lasted for ten minutes, then ceased, to be followed by that strange inarticulate sigh of weariness which ever succeeds the heavy bombardment. Ten minutes is a short time, but an eternity under shell fire. And when the storm died away, Jules was lying on the trench floor in a widening pool of his own blood, with a gaping hole in his chest. Ninette was beside him with a lump of shrapnel through her lungs.

In a short space of time the shambles were cleared, and when midnight approached Jules and Ninette were lying side by side in the cellar of a ruined farmhouse half a mile back, and Jules was dying. It was an advanced dressing station, and Ninette's secret had been discovered when her wounds were dressed; but the kind-hearted surgeon had heard her gasped-out story, and had placed their mud-spattered, blood-smeared stretchers side by side in a corner near the doorway. For one glance at Jules had told him that nothing mattered now. Once, as he passed along to look at another case, Ninette looked up and asked him what hour it was; and the surgeon told her as he moved on. It was midnight.

With an effort Ninette raised herself on her elbow and bent over the dying man.

"Jules, mon Jules," she whispered. "It is midnight; do you hear the angels?"

And Jules turned on her his wearied eyes, eyes already glazed with the cold chill of death. A radiance seemed to spread over the pale, pain-racked face—

"I hear them," he muttered drowsily; "I hear them, Ninette . . . Ninette . . . adieu!"

Perhaps she heard them, too; for as she leaned over and kissed the blue, parted lips, something within her made her heart leap, despite the aching sense of loneliness and of loss, and the sure knowledge that her world of dreams and visions of the home with Jules was vanished now and passed away . . . and, low and tenderly, she said, "Jules, mon ami . . . ne disons pas adieu—mais au revoir."

* * * * *

They carried him out later—there is no room for the dead where the living claim. But as the surgeon worked on at the intermittent flow of sagging stretchers no one noticed that one lay empty by the corner at the door, or that a diminutive form had crept from the dim cellar. Ninette, faint and half stupid from pain and loss of blood, had followed her Jules as they carried him and two other inert and lifeless bodies out into the courtyard and round to the back of the house. And, supporting herself against a poplar tree which rose from a thick undergrowth of wooden crosses, she watched four men rapidly digging a grave by the dim light of a shaded lantern. Soon they finished the shallow hole, lifted the three bodies and laid them side by side. A tall figure, muffled in a greatcoat, mumbled the last rites; and in a few minutes the earth had covered that which of mortal destiny must return unto dust. The men stretched themselves; one yawned heavily . . . another man lit a cigarette, extinguished the lantern, and Ninette heard their footsteps stumbling away round the corner of the farmhouse.

Then she crawled forward and knelt by the mound which covered Jules—her Jules. She neither sobbed nor wept, for life itself for Ninette was laid beneath that earth. And when it comes to that, the human heart is beyond tears. She merely gazed into the blackness and called "Jules." Then she lay down across that grave and found the mercy of oblivion.

Later it rained, and the poplar dripped, but Ninette slept on. And the raindrops fell upon her softly, but she waked not . . .

And when in the morning they found her there perhaps she was with Jules, and it had only been au revoir after all; for the day broke clear and glorious in opalescent light through the cloven clouds on the Eastern sky.

IN THIS NUMBER ——

You will find a Christmas Greeting written for us by Miss Katharine Tynan, the famous Irish poetess and novelist. Autographed by Queen Alexandra, Princess Arthur of Connaught, and many great ladies; the M.S. of a song by Second-Lieut. Ivor Novello—composer of "Keep the Home Fires Burning," "Theodore and Co.," &c.—and contributions in prose and verse by "Yeo," author of "Soldier Men"; Charles L. Warr, author of "Echoes From Flanders"; R. M. Eassie, author of "Odes to Trifles"; and Coningsby Dawson, author of "Khaki Courage."

"My doctor told me I should have to leave off eating so much meat."

"Did you laugh at him?"

"I did at first, but when he sent in his bill I found that he was right."

GOOD FOOD GONE TO WAIST.

Spr. C. Taylor, R.O.D., R.E.

Bill: "ONLY THREE MISSIONARIES IN THE SOLOMON ISLANDS TO NINETY THOUSAND CANNIBALS, BOB."
Bob: "WHY, THE POOR BEGGARS'LL STARVE!" *F. S. and Lieut. Trevelyan, H.M.S. Imperieuse.*

TO THE GIRLS WE LEFT BEHIND.

By the Author of "Khaki Courage."

Each night we panted till the runners came,
  Bearing your letters through the battle-smoke;
Their path lay up Death Valley spouting flame,
  Across the ridge where the Hun's anger spoke
In bursting shells and cataracts of pain;
  Then down the road where no one goes by day,
And so into the tortured, pock-marked plain,
  Where dead men clasp their wounds and point the way.
Here gas lurks treacherously and the wire
  Of old defences tangles up the foot;
Faces and hands strain upward through the mire
  Speaking the anguish of the Hun retreat.
Some nights no letters came; the evening hate
  Dragged on till dawn. The ridge in flying spray
Of hissing shrapnel told the runners' fate;
  We knew we should not hear from you that day—
From you brave girls we each have left behind,
  Who, while you smile, struggle with sobbing breath
And write your souls on paper to be kind.
  To know you love us takes the sting from death.

    (Lieut.) CONINGSBY DAWSON.

A VOICE.

Ah! beautiful mother, how wondrous you are,
In the eyes of this soldier who's fighting afar;
Who hears your soft voice, yet who hears not a sound
Save the crashing of guns and the hell all around;
Who sees your sweet smile, yet there's nothing at all,
For memory painted it—then let it fall
Into the roar of the battle—to drown.
Ah! dearest of mothers, how watchful you are
To the ways of this soldier whose fighting afar.

For you are the greatest of all things out here,
To the heart of this soldier who's lonely and drear.
Do you know that he turns from the turmoil and strife,
And thinks of, and loves you, and prays for his life
That he may return home and tell you some day
Of the thoughts which he failed to when he went away.
How you peep at him sadly from out of the night,
Or sit in his dug-out—then slip from his sight.
Oh! wonderful mother, what comfort you are
To the soul of this soldier who's fighting afar.

But God sent an angel, and now he's on leave,
In that beautiful haven, which waits to receive
That vast army of heroes who lay down their lives
For the sake of their children, their homesteads and wives;
For the sake of their king and their country and all,
And there in the glory they wait for the call
Of God's martial order, which brings to them there
Their mothers on earth who have no one to care.
Oh! be rested, dear mothers, brave mothers you are;
You shall come to your loved ones in the New World afar.

    Capt. D. CRAIG-JOHNSON.

SONNET.

Against our England's deathless soul has rolled,
As waves that vainly wash her rocky coast,
The lustful myriads of an armèd host,
With panoply of horror. To withhold
Their frenzied rush, the boldest o' the bold
Have ta'en up arms to-day, not counting cost;
Our men have dared to face the holocaust,
And dared t'endure till Death has struck them cold!
Master of Nations! What might not Thy hand
From such brave fabric fashion for the earth?
Guide thou, with steady touch and sure, our way,
Lift up the eyes of those that rule our land,
From selfish aims to things of truer worth;
So shall we move towards Eternal Day!

UNPRESCRIBED TREATMENT.

Arthur Ferrier after Sapper C. Marr, R.E.

Officer: "RATHER A STRANGE CROWD, SERGEANT."
Sergeant (disgustedly): "YESSIR—BATCH OF RECRUITS FROM HEADQUARTERS, SIR—LOOK AT 'EM—A BLOOMING MORSE CODE!"
A. G. Vandersyde, A.S.C.

"IT'S ALL RIGHT NOW, BILL! YOU CAN COME OUT—THERE AIN'T ANY MORE COMING!"
Dr. E. J. S. Hall, A.S.C.

"THREE STARS AND AN M.C."

THE CAPTAIN'S REPORT.

BREVITY is the distinguishing note of the answer recently returned by a Captain (with the B.E.F.) to the straight question, What advantages have you gained from Pelmanism?

His reply was:—

"Three Stars,
A Military Cross, and
A Clearer Head."

Concise and emphatic! He is not the only officer who has frankly attributed his "honours" to Pelmanism, and there are hundreds of officers who place their promotion to the credit of this remarkable system of mind-training. A Lieut.-Colonel states that his promotion was "a direct consequence" of what he had gained from Lesson 2; whilst the Captain of a fine cruiser records the gratifying fact that he was promoted to his command, *not* by seniority but as a result of Pelmanism. A Major, again, thanks the Pelman System for his D.S.O.

And these cases are literally typical of hundreds. **An entire issue of "Punch" could very easily be filled simply with letters from naval and military officers who have written to the Pelman Institute to express their thanks for the benefit derived from the Course.** Scepticism in face of overwhelming evidence would be folly.

It is this unanswerable logic of facts which has so completely broken down prejudice. In the early days—when "Pelmanism" was a comparatively unknown factor—one naturally hesitated to take the published statements "on faith." Mr. George R. Sims recently wrote that he accepted them *cum grano salis*—until he found, upon investigation, that there was no exaggeration whatever. A London Solicitor even goes so far as to say, "I used to think the claims made for Pelmanism must be fantastic: **now I consider them to be understatement of the truth.**

The Natural Sequel.

Others had the same experience. The consequence is that to-day there are 37 Generals, 6 Admirals, over 300 Colonels and Naval Captains, and nearly 4,000 other officers!—making with N.C.O.'s and men 10,000 on active service who are practising Pelmanism.

These facts are amazing to those who have no knowledge of the System. But a very slight acquaintance with it satisfies one that there is not an officer of H.M. Army or Navy who would not be well-advised to take the Pelman course.

A very well-known General quite recently sent one of his staff-officers to enrol: the General had only got through a *quarter of the Course* at that time. Quite a large number of Commanders have paid the Pelman Course a similar compliment.

Business Men and "Pelmanism."

It is the same in the business world. Here, of course, financial ambitions are the primary motive. Many men (and women) have reported 100 per cent., 200 per cent., 300 per cent., **and even greater** increases of income due to the adoption of Pelmanism. The ultimate object is different, but the road is the same—Efficiency. Pelmanism has brought that ancient shibboleth into the realm of practical politics.

Here is a striking case, quite a typical one. A large Midland firm caused one of their head men to enrol for the Pelman Course a few months ago. His progress was noted carefully, the result being that within three months eight members of the firm applied for enrolment, including the Managing Director, Secretary, Works Manager, etc.

"TRUTH'S" Verdict.

"TRUTH" made the work of the Pelman Institute the subject of a searching inquiry. The fearlessly critical attitude of the famous journal makes its judgment valuable to the entire English-speaking world.

"TRUTH'S" opinion is significantly summarised in the following sentence:—

"The advice which sends a student to the Pelman Institute is not likely to be regretted either by him who gives or by him who takes it, since it is founded on an honest conclusion drawn from indisputable facts." ("TRUTH," May 30, 1917.)

A Student of the Course recently wrote: "If people only knew, the doors of the Pelman Institute would be literally besieged by eager applicants." Even as a purely social and intellectual factor, Pelmanism well repays the few hours required for its study. As a 'Varsity man wrote:—

"It inculcates a clean, thorough, courageous method of playing the game of Life—admirably suited to the English Temperament, and should prove *moral* salvation to many a business man. 'Success,' too, would follow—but I consider this as secondary."

Qualities Developed.

Following the intensely interesting lessons and exercises, the students of Pelmanism rapidly develop a brilliant Memory, strong Will Power, complete power of Concentration, quick Decision, sound Judgment, an ability to reason clearly, to Converse attractively, to Organise and Manage, and to conduct their work and social duties with Tact, Courage, Self-Confidence, and Success. All mental weaknesses and defects are, on the other hand, eliminated—such as Mind-wandering, Forgetfulness, Weak Will, Aimlessness, Bashfulness, Self-consciousness, the "Worry Habit," etc., etc. The Course is taught entirely by post, and all correspondence is strictly confidential.

The Directors of the Institute have arranged a substantial reduction in the fee to enable readers of "Blighty" to secure the complete course with a minimum outlay.

To get the benefit of this liberal offer application should be made at once by post card or by letter to the address below.

A full description of the Pelman Course is given in "Mind and Memory," a free copy of which (together with "TRUTH'S" special Report on "Pelmanism," and particulars showing how to secure the Course for one-third less than the usual fee) will be sent post free to all readers of "Blighty" who send to The Pelman Institute, 2, Wenham House, Bloomsbury Street, London, W.C. 1.

Overseas Addresses: 46, Market Street, Melbourne. 15, Toronto Street, Toronto. Club Arcade, Durban.

The Motor-Car was first introduced into Britain by the Phœnicians, who came from Tyre. They brought these machines to barter in exchange for "tin."

There will be no need to barter for the Post-War "Austin" 20-h.p. Car, as the price will be popular and the quality fully up to "Austin" standard.

Makers of Private & Commercial Motor Cars.

Aircraft and Aircraft Engines.

Petrol & Paraffin Electric Generating Plants, &c., &c.

Head Office and Works:
NORTHFIELD, BIRMINGHAM

Branches at
LONDON, MANCHESTER, NORWICH, PARIS.

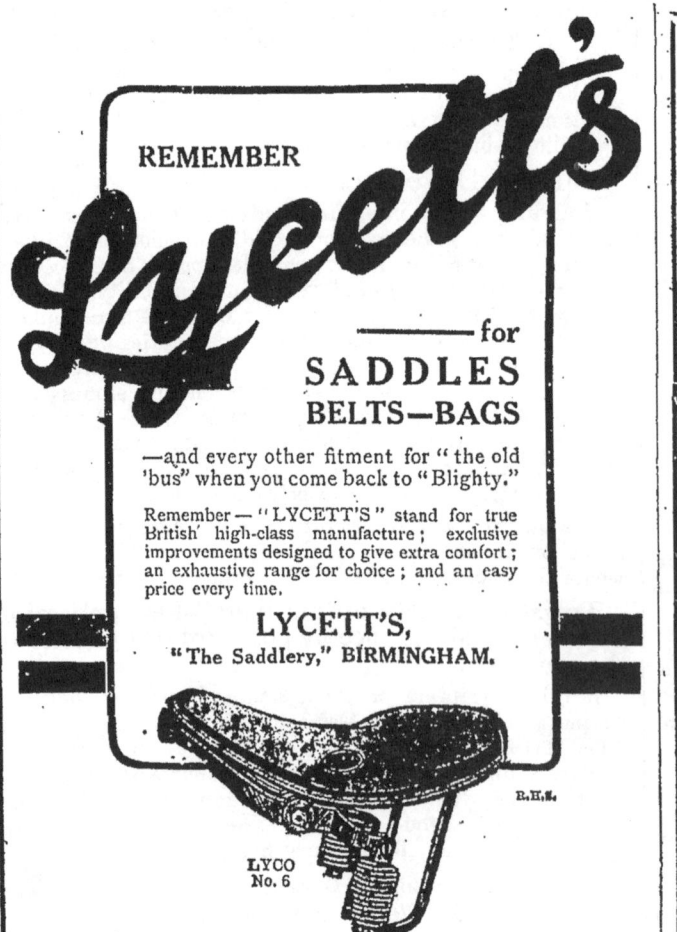

REMEMBER **Lycett's** for SADDLES BELTS—BAGS

—and every other fitment for "the old 'bus" when you come back to "Blighty."

Remember — "LYCETT'S" stand for true British high-class manufacture; exclusive improvements designed to give extra comfort; an exhaustive range for choice; and an easy price every time.

LYCETT'S,
"The Saddlery," BIRMINGHAM.

LYCO No. 6

Furniture Town CRIER

Monthly Bargain List free on request. XMAS No.

ROADS.

Roads were invented for the purpose of quick transit. After a time they got so full up that roads were made under the roads. At one time all roads led to Rome. Now they lead to Jelks' and Home.
You can see everything on the roads, men, women, children, Fords and Jelks' Vans.
Most of the men, women, children and Fords are going to Jelks'. Jelks' Vans are taking Furniture to the Homes of the men, women, and children.

Jelks' have 250,000 square feet of the Holloway Road and

£50,000 *worth of* HIGH-GRADE SECOND-HAND FURNITURE

On those square feet. Come along the road with the crowd and see the bargains at pre-war prices.

TERMS: CASH OR EASY PAYMENTS.

W. JELKS & SONS,
263—275,
Holloway Rd., London, N.7.

BUSINESS HOURS:
9—8.
THURSDAYS: 9—1 P.M.
SATURDAYS: 9—9.

'Bus, Tram or Tube (Pic.) to door.

Sergt.-Major (at Training Area): "WHY THE BLAZES DID YOU FIRE AFTER I GAVE THE 'CEASE FIRE'?"
Just Out From England: "OH, IT'S ALL RIGHT, SIR—IT WOULDN'T GO VERY FAR."
"WHAT D'YOU MEAN BY 'WOULDN'T GO VERY FAR'?"
"WHY, I DIDN'T PULL IT *very* HARD, SIR."

Sgt. T. Crewe, 6th East Yorks.

Tommy (whose shaving has been interrupted and glass smashed): "I KNEW IT—NO LUCK FOR SEVEN YEARS!"

Pte. N. Kirby, R.A.M.C.

"BABY DOESN'T SEEM TO KNOW ME."
"WELL, YOU SEE, MRS. JONES, I TOOK HIM TO THE ZOO YESTERDAY, AND ONE OF THE MONKEYS FRIGHTENED HIM."
A. M. and Phil Lawford, 1/1 Sherwood Rgrs. Yeo.

Instructor: "WHEN YER MAKES YER POINT WITH THE BAYONET, GRIND YER TEETH, ROLL YER EYES, AND GIT THE WIND UP 'IM, SEE?"
Recruit: "RIGHT YOU ARE, NOBBY, BUT LEND US YOUR FICE!"
A. M. and L/cpl. L. Mosley, 4th Sherwoods.

Extract from Letter Home: "WHEN THERE IS ANYTHING ON, I AM ALWAYS CERTAIN TO BE PRETTY NEAR IT."
Pte. Percy Cannot, 11th Corps Hd. Qrs.

THE RETORT OBVIOUS.

Pte. Stylo (late Hand-cuff King from the Halls): "GENTLEMEN! IN LESS THAN TWENTY SECONDS, I WILL BE AMONG YOU."

Pte. A. Knight, 9th K.O. Royal Lancs.

Veterinary Officer (examining men on horse management): "NOW, ABOUT THE TREATMENT OF FEET; IF A HORSE HAD FOUR BAD FEET, WHAT WOULD YOU DO?"
Old Hand: "INDENT FOR A NEW 'ORSE, SIR."

Pte. F. Sherwin, 2/H.A.C.

Triplex Safety Glass

"Triplex" for Aeroplane Goggles, Windshields and Observation Panels.

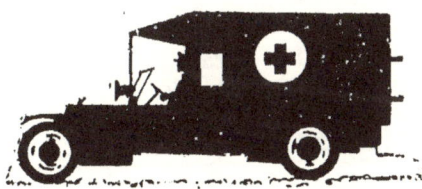

"Triplex" for Windows and Windscreens of Red Cross Vans, Transports, &c.

"Triplex" for Goggles for Despatch Riders, &c.

"Triplex" for the Portholes of Warships, Merchant Vessels and Passenger Liners.

O.H.M.S.

"Triplex" Safety Glass is doing its bit at home and at the front by saving the sight and even the lives of Aviators, Motor-Transport Drivers, &c. This wonderful glass, whilst being outwardly indistinguishable from ordinary glass, is absolutely unsplinterable. It can be cracked, but no particle can become detached.

"Triplex" should be used in *all* cases where glass is required, because it is the *only* Safety Glass.

An Ideal Xmas Gift
for *your* Soldier, whether he be an Airman, Despatch Rider or Motor Transport Driver, is—
A Pair of "Triplex" Goggles.

Investigate Triplex. Catalogue free on request.

THE "TRIPLEX" SAFETY GLASS CO., LTD.,
1, ALBEMARLE ST., PICCADILLY, LONDON, W. 1.

Telephone: REGENT 1340.
Telegrams: "SHATTERLYS, PICCY, LONDON."

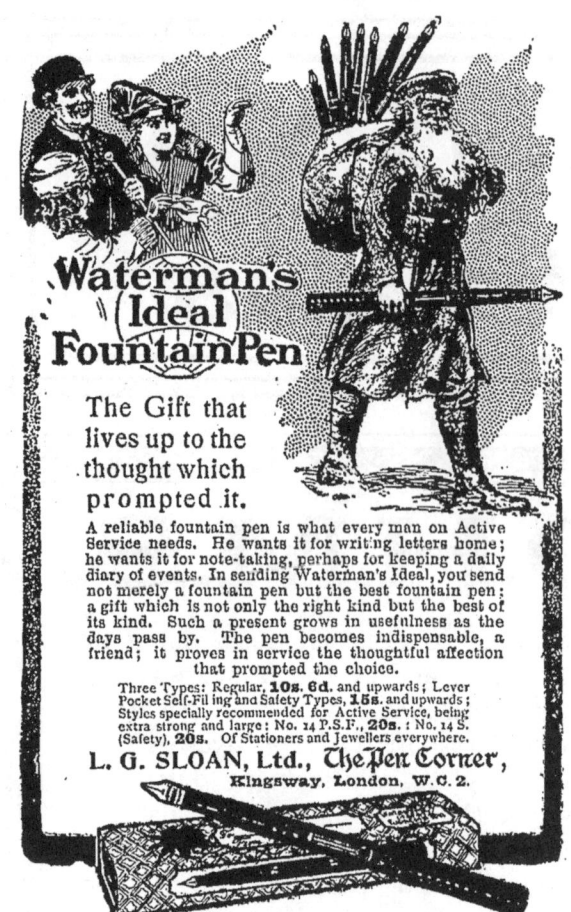

Waterman's Ideal Fountain Pen

The Gift that lives up to the thought which prompted it.

A reliable fountain pen is what every man on Active Service needs. He wants it for writing letters home; he wants it for note-taking, perhaps for keeping a daily diary of events. In sending Waterman's Ideal, you send not merely a fountain pen but the best fountain pen; a gift which is not only the right kind but the best of its kind. Such a present grows in usefulness as the days pass by. The pen becomes indispensable, a friend; it proves in service the thoughtful affection that prompted the choice.

Three Types: Regular, **10s. 6d.** and upwards; Lever Pocket Self-Filing and Safety Types, **15s.** and upwards; Styles specially recommended for Active Service, being extra strong and large: No. 14 P.S.F., **20s.**: No. 14 S. (Safety), **20s.** Of Stationers and Jewellers everywhere.

L. G. SLOAN, Ltd., The Pen Corner,
Kingsway, London, W.C.2.

THE IDEAL GIFT.

Of all the lovely things in the range of gems there is none that rivals the pearl. Nothing gives more constant pleasure to a lady, be she wife, fiancée, daughter, sister, or friend. A beautiful Ciro Pearl Necklet, Brooch, Ring, or any jewel with Ciro Pearls is the ideal gift. Each jewel is fitted in a beautiful case which gives it a real cachet.

CIRO PEARLS
Are a new Scientific Discovery.

THE most wonderful reproduction of genuine pearls ever brought before the public.

Pearls which possess the identical weight, sheen and orient of genuine pearls, but at a price that is within the reach of the most modest purse.

CIRO PEARLS are sold at one price only. Whether a gorgeous string of pearls—graduated or otherwise, a ring, a brooch, a pair of earrings, or any jewel, designs of which appear in our booklet, which we will send on request, no matter what size pearl you require you need not ask the price; each article is sold at £1 1 0. The mountings are as exquisite as if the pearls were genuine, and the pearls superior to anything yet produced at any price.

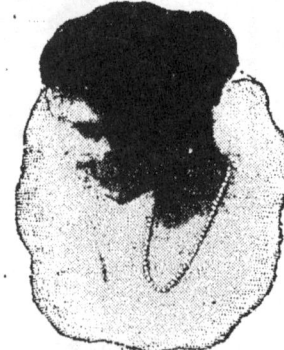

Reproduction of Ciro Pearl Necklet at £1 1 0, including beautiful case.

In order to convince you of the superiority of Ciro Pearls over all others, regardless of their price, and also to prove to you that experts are deceived by them although they cost but £1 1 0, we make you the most unique and liberal offer ever made.

We will send you a Necklace, a Ring, or any of our Jewels, on receipt of £1 1 0. Wear either for a week. Compare them with the finest of genuine pearls or the highest price artificial pearls. If you are not satisfied, or if your friends can tell it is not real, return it to us and we will refund you your money in full.

Isn't it a satisfaction to buy your Xmas gifts from a firm whose confidence is so completely expressed? You are at least assured that you are getting the best value money can buy.

If you cannot call at our Showrooms post your order to the
CIRO SCIENTIFIC PEARL CO., Ltd.,
(Dept. 112) 42, Piccadilly, W. 1,
when it shall have our intelligent careful service.

"BEAUTIFULLY COOL AND SWEET SMOKING."

PLAYER'S NAVY CUT TOBACCO

Packed in varying degrees of strength to suit every class of smoker.

	Per oz.
Player's Gold Leaf Navy Cut	
Player's Medium Navy Cut	8½d.
Player's Tawny Navy Cut	
PLAYER'S "WHITE LABEL" NAVY CUT	7½d.

Also Player's **Navy Cut de Luxe** (a development of Player's Navy Cut) packed in Airtight Tins.

2-oz. Tins   **1/9**      **4-oz. Tins**   **3/6**

PLAYER'S NAVY CUT CIGARETTES

Have a world-wide reputation. They are made from fine quality Virginia Tobacco and sold in two strengths—Mild and Medium.

MILD (Gold Leaf)   **MEDIUM**

100 for 4/6	50 for 2/3	100 for 3/5	50 for 1/9½
24 for 1/1	12 for 6½d.	20 for 8½d.	10 for 4½d.

IN PACKETS AND TINS FROM ALL TOBACCONISTS AND STORES.
These Cigarettes (and Tobaccos) are also supplied at **DUTY FREE RATES** for the purpose of gratuitous distribution to wounded Soldiers and Sailors in Hospital.

Terms and particulars on application to— **JOHN PLAYER and SONS, Nottingham.**
Branch of the Imperial Tobacco Co. (of Great Britain and Ireland), Ltd.

Tommy (to Escort with prisoner wearing body shield): "WHO'S YER FRIEND, MATE—JOAN OF ARC?"
Escort: "DUNNO—BUT IF YOU'LL LEND ME A TIN OPENER, I'LL HAVE A LOOK AT ITS IDENTITY DISC."

W. Smithson Broadhead.

THE FINAL TEST.

UNFIT.

Sapper C. Marr, 180 Co., R.E.

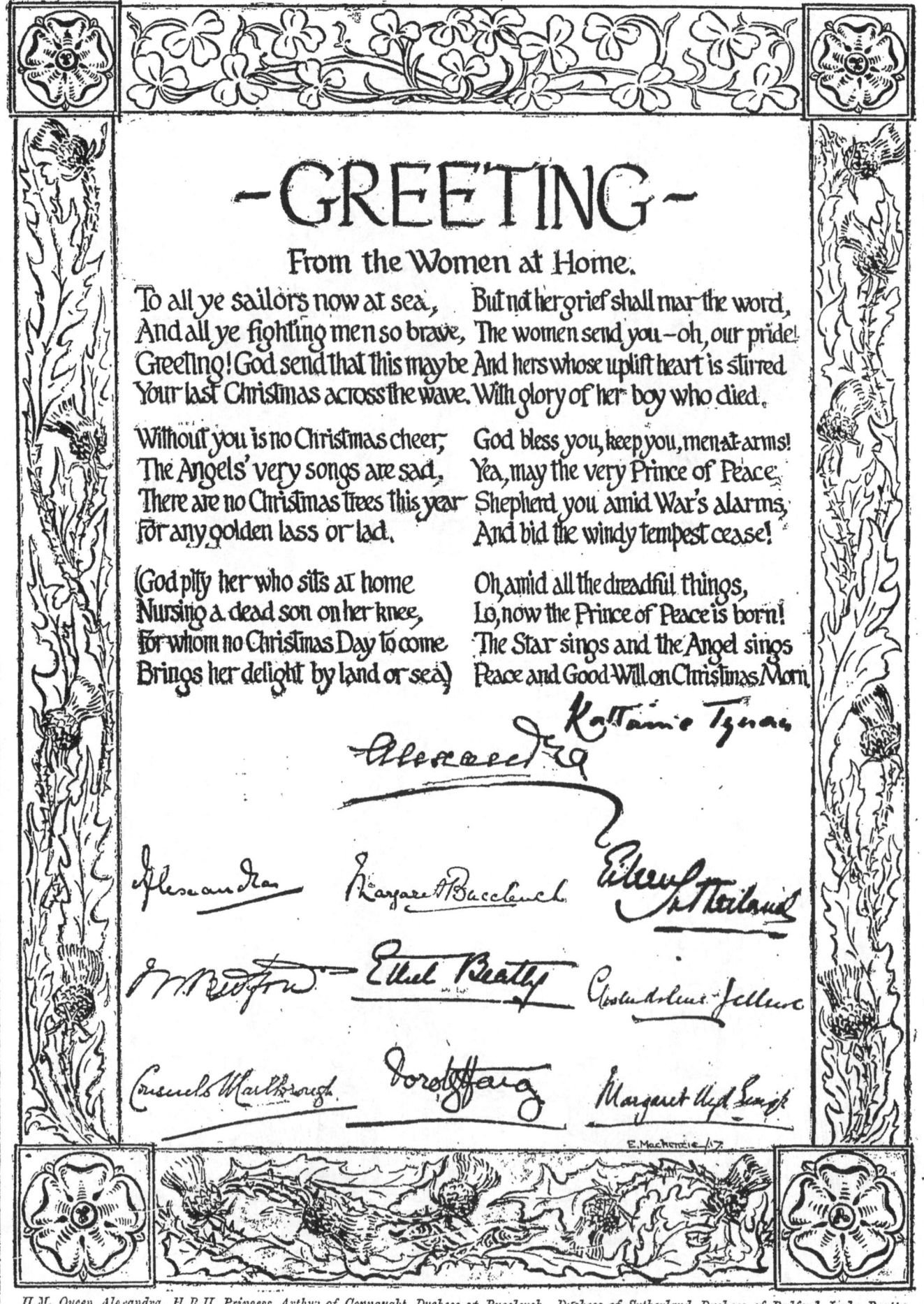

GREETING
From the Women at Home.

To all ye sailors now at sea,
And all ye fighting men so brave,
Greeting! God send that this may be
Your last Christmas across the wave.

Without you is no Christmas cheer,
The Angels' very songs are sad,
There are no Christmas trees this year
For any golden lass or lad.

(God pity her who sits at home
Nursing a dead son on her knee,
For whom no Christmas Day to come
Brings her delight by land or sea)

But not her grief shall mar the word,
The women send you—oh, our pride!
And hers whose uplift heart is stirred
With glory of her boy who died.

God bless you, keep you, men-at-arms!
Yea, may the very Prince of Peace,
Shepherd you amid War's alarms,
And bid the windy tempest cease!

Oh, amid all the dreadful things,
Lo, now the Prince of Peace is born!
The Star sings and the Angel sings
Peace and Good-Will on Christmas Morn.

H.M. Queen Alexandra, H.R.H. Princess Arthur of Connaught, Duchess of Buccleuch, Duchess of Sutherland, Duchess of Bedford, Lady Beatty, Lady Jellicoe, Duchess of Marlborough, Lady Haig, Mrs. Lloyd George. Verses: Katharine Tynan. Decoration: E. Mackenzie, late 1/4 Seaforths.

THEIR FIRST MEETING.

Rip, after Lt. Hill, Canadians.

"JOCK'S BAUN'."

Contrary to our expectations Christmas Day dawned clear and rainless, a weak, watery sun shining dully on the snow-clad strip of shell-marked ground which separated us from the Huns.

You will, no doubt, remember how, on the first war Christmas, we spent an enjoyable time fraternising (description à la press). That means to say that we visited their trenches and told them what we thought of them, and explained in detail our intentions for the following spring. Perhaps it is just as well that they did not understand English. On the second year we each made a strafe during the forenoon, the intensity of which rapidly died to a nonentity after our Christmas dinner of rum and biscuits had been dished out and consumed. The third year we strafed all day and part of the night as well, just to show the Huns that the friendly spirit in which we had undertaken to teach them a lesson had not diminished with the years.

The menu for this, the fourth Christmas Day, commenced with shrapnel flavoured with aircraft pepper, included an unsavoury course from the gas detachment, and concluded with some nasty remarks by the Light Artillery section, who nobly upheld the traditions of festival speech-making by continuing for five hours at a stretch.

Old Jock (our "Burgoo" sergeant), however, considered this insufficient, and thought that something special ought to be arranged to celebrate his fourth Christmas in the trenches. We unanimously agreed that something unusual should be served for supper, and chuckled with delight as Jock unfolded his plans. As a result, during the afternoon lull I crept along to the Gordons' section and borrowed McTavish, their piper, for that evening. Smith called on the Munsters and secured the services of Malone, their big-drum expert, Jones paid a friendly visit to the Artillery section, and returned with sufficient bombs for the duration of the war (I'm not an optimistic person), and old Jock, by a skilful distribution of rum he had unearthed from the ruins of a transport waggon, secured the services of McWhachal and McGinty, both "civvy" pals of his, the former a Trombonist Kilty with ambition and a tutor which had, so far, only been opened at the first page, the latter, the genial corporal of the new "Melesha," who would undoubtedly have proved a Paganini amongst cornettists had he known how to play it.

Darkness saw our little band, loaded to the neck with "startlers," creeping along one of the advanced saps to an unpleasant accompaniment from the opposite artillery.

Jock gave us our orders as we progressed. "The Baun'," he said, "will gang in front after leavin' their bombs in a handy spot so that we can easily get them if oor ain supply rins oot. When I gie the word, they will stert wi' 'The Campbells are Coming' as lood as they can blaw, followin' up wi' 'Wha' saw the Forty Second,' an' 'Tipperary,' an' keep it up until I gie the order tae retire. The bombin' section will follow at the rear until close enough tae render their selections. I will imitate a coo wha' has lost her calf, Smithie will howl as though he had waukened in the middle o' the nicht an' fun' a ghost below the bed, Jones can mak' that row he caws singin', an' you (that's me) can dae onything ye like sae lang as it adds tae the din."

Unfortunately the Huns took it into their heads to give a firework display just then, and we were forced to lie low, in a mucky shell hole at that, for nearly half an hour. After that had subsided it was easy going until we had arrived within ten yards of their trenches. The Huns were singing "Once we were at Paris, now we're going home," and did not suspect anything in the nature of the free entertainment we had arranged.

"Right!" howled Jock. Then followed a most unearthly din, worse even than the explosion of the mines at Messines, or the ructions which follow a Ramsay MacDonald peace meeting. McTavish kicked up a devilish row, McWhachal's trombone blared like an overstrung fog horn, McGinty's cornet shrieked unceasingly as he made a realistic attempt to blow his lungs out, and Malone's drum made more row than a thousand guns firing simultaneously. Whilst the vocal section rained bombs along the line, they rendered their turns most effectively, Jock's imitation of the "coo" almost drowning the shrieks of Smithie as he thought of a ghost tickling his feet in the middle of the night. Jones sang most beautifully —and vociferously, and I added to the din by howling like a kid who has lost her "polk" (cribbed from Jock) at a Sunday School soiree.

The Huns wondered what on earth had struck them, and fell like ninepins as our bombs burst amongst them. Right along the line we progressed, raining bombs and sustaining the row as we went, until Jock eventually gave the word to cease fire.

"Tak' yer spoil," he howled, and immediately rounded up a crowd of gibbering "sausages" who were cowering terror-stricken in a corner of the trench. Swiftly we gathered all in the vicinity and herded them across to our lines, where, after divesting them of helmets, medals, and other little souvenirs, we counted our haul. The total amounted to twenty-five, not a bad haul considering hundreds we had "outed" with our bombs, and the thousands who had died of fright.

As we are extremely modest persons, the remarks passed by the brigadier when he heard of our little expedition, will not be included in this report, but it will do no harm to quote a paragraph which appeared originally in the leader of one of the foremost German dailies, apparently compiled by the German Belloc.

"The shortage of British manpower can be further proved by an incident which occurred on Christmas Day. As is usual, our troops had ceased hostilities and were holding quiet Christmas celebrations, lulled into a sense of false security by the barbarous British, when thousands of howling savages, presumably from the wilds of Timbuctoo, raided our front line trenches. Although our gallant troops were completely taken by surprise, we repulsed the enemy with heavy loss. No further attack was made."

I must include the remarks made by Jock when he read this.

"Savages frae Timbuctoo," he said. "A'll teach them tae ca' me a savage. A'll show them that a come frae Scotland, the only undefeated country in the world, or ma name isna' Jock McTavish."

As those Jocks have a nasty habit (for the Germans) of sticking to their word if it relates in any way to fighting, you may expect to hear further startling news in the "savage" line in the near future with further "heavy loss."

JOHN M. COCKBURN,
H.M.S. Gibraltar.

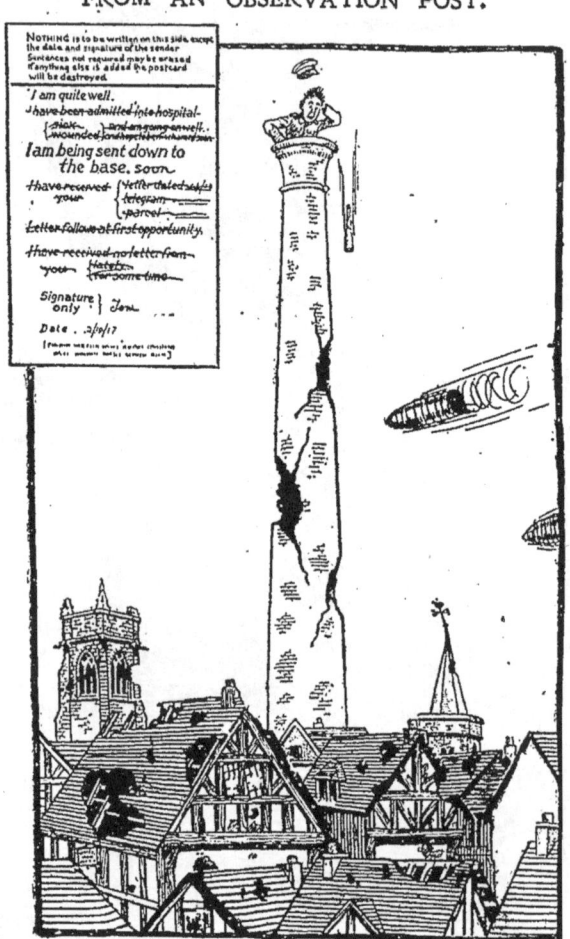

FROM AN OBSERVATION POST.

Rfn. F. Exton, 2/6th King's Liverpool Rgt.

THE COMFORTER.

Kitty (encouragingly, to her intended about to return to the Front): "NOW, JIM, do CHEER UP; YOUR LITTLE GIRL WILL BE TRUE TO YOU EVEN IF YOU DON'T GET LEAVE AGAIN FOR FIFTY YEARS."
Cpl. J. C. Walker, R.E.

ON SAYING GOOD-BYE TO MY LONELINESS.

By A LONELY SOLDIER.

The waiting hours between the strafes,
   When others read their "billet doos,"
And swopped with sniggerings and laughs,
   The items of each other's "noos";
But never came a single line
   From any breathing soul I knew,
To say, "Old man, I'm doing fine,
   And how the dismal deuce are you?"
I got so lonely that I grew
   Gladly to welcome a stand-to.

The boredom of the dreary night,
   In damp dug-out and candleless;
How vain my efforts were to fight
   And conquer my covetousness;
I got to hate to take my share
   Of other's smokes and home-made cake,
They never thought it so unfair
   That they should give and I should take;
   I used to think the time dragged slow
   Till my turn came for sentry-go.

Then one fine day there came those socks
   (They were not really meant for me),
But Fate directed that the box
   Should be addressed illegibly;
And deep down in the toe of one
   I found a hasty scribbled note,
"Write to the sender just for fun,"
   And so I did, but what I wrote—
I didn't like to make it long
   And felt afraid to pitch it strong.

And so I saw her on my leave;
   I tell you, between you and me,
You never, never, could believe
   That there was such a girl as she;
How every memr'y still remains
   Of hours I sprawled upon the sands,
Or lingered in those Sussex lanes
   Learning to hold a woman's hands:
Just now nobody hears me boast
I'm keen to go on list'ning post.

And so, farewell my loneliness,
   I rather think you did me good,
I rather think 'twas more or less,
   Because of you I understood,
And so, my dragging hours farewell,
   I thank you that you did me proud,
When teaching me that one is hell,
   To prove to me that three's a crowd.
And *le bon Dieu* knows what to do
   When it is just a case of two.
          R. M. EASSIE,
     Author of "Odes to Trifles."

YOUTH AND AGE.

Now, youth is youth, and age is age,
   And if ever the twain do meet,
The converse which follows is passing strange,
   And ofttimes far from sweet.
For youth is honest, but age is—wise
   And demands belief as its right.
Which honesty gives, but with grudging hand,
   When facts are improving its sight.
"Young man, you have shown the Prussian horde
   That we do not fear their might;
And if I were of age to bear the sword,
   I should be with you in the fight.
Oh! what a blessing it is to be young,
   Able, and fit for the strife:
To fight, and to die, just in honour's cause,
   Gad! Sir! 'Tis a glorious life.

"Yes, I've read the news of each battle fought,
   And waved my flag with the rest.
I've sat on committees of every kind,
   And done my bit with the best.
But I wish my age were twenty years less,
   And that I could enjoy the fun
Of the stirring fight, and the glory gained,
   And the record of honour won."

The soldier took his pipe from his mouth,
   And said with a cynical grin:
"You're talking as if you would like the game;
   But—you're out of it—and I'm in.
And if I had only twenty years more,
   I'd be talking the same as you;
But still, as it is, the sooner it's o'er,
   The better I'm pleased, and that's true.

"There isn't much fun in living in mud,
   Nor in dodging a German shell.
When you've done talking and come to the point,
   Well, war is precisely—Pure Hell.
You talk pretty big 'bout being too old,
   Well, if you my opinion should seek,
It is this: If you're too d——d old to fight,
   Well, you're too d——d old to speak.
          Sapper H. N. SYMES.

THE BRIDGE ACROSS THE STREAM.

Specially composed for "Blighty."

BY IVOR NOVELLO (Sub-Lieut., R.N.V.R.)
(Composer of the famous "Till the Boys Come Home.")

Words by J. E. MacManus.

I.
I mind the meadows waving,
  When the breeze was warm in June;
And the song the woods were singing,
  Of the summer all in tune.
The trees gave just a whisper,
  And the birds were half asleep;
But the air was full of music
  That murmured soft and deep.

Refrain:
And the bridge was where we waited
  Till our sweetheart came along.
With her smile as bright as summer,
  And her voice as soft as song.
We're far from home and country,
  Old times seem like a dream,
But the girls we love will wait for us
  On the bridge across the stream.

II.
It was cool beneath the shadows
  Where the drooping branches fell,
And the sound of rippling waters
  Was like a silver bell.
You could see the blue sky mirrored
  When the pools were deep and calm.
It was grand to be alive and young,
  And we didn't care a dalm.

Copyright, 1917, by Ascherberg, Hopwood and Crew, Ltd., 16, Mortimer Street, London, W.

Copies of this song, published in ordinary form, can be had from all music dealers at 1s. 8d. net, or post free 1s. 9d. from the publishers as above.

A NEW DRILL.

Sir,—Is there any truth in the rumour that a new drill called the "Eating Drill" is shortly to be introduced into the army? It runs something like this:—

Eating Drill as a complete practice. Both ranks sitting facing inwards, or otherwise so disposed as suits time and place. Neckwear and belts to be loosened.

On the word "One" plunge the fork into the object to be eaten, at the same time drop the lower jaw to the full extent and remain steady.

On the word "Two" raise the object thus impaled in a circular motion, elbows close to the sides, thumb close to the forefinger, eyes straight to the front, mouth with an expectant look of food.

"ON THE WORD 'TWO.'"

"TILL THE APPETITE IS SATISFIED."

No "slobbering" allowed, care being taken not to distribute the condiments or gravy on your neighbour's uniform.

On the word "Three" let me hear those lower jaws come together with a "click."

On the word "Four" bring the hand and fork and jaw smartly back to position "one."

"As you were." Repeat the operation till the appetite is satisfied, or till the contents of the plate are finished, or whichever is less.

For the purposes of the drill, dummy corks, duly numbered, will be served out to the Battalion to take the place of the impaled object. When proficiency is attained, extra rations will be served out from the canteen fund on review days.

Note.—N.C.O.'s and privates' corks must be kept separate.

Lt.-Col. A. POPE.

MICKY AND THE GENERAL.

When I looked in to tell Micky the news, I found him just about to start on his temporary duty of sweeping out the "bivvys" (meaning "bivouac"). A kindly-disposed mule had presented him with a kick which had been just hard enough to necessitate Micky going sick and "swinging it" to the extent of three days "L.D." (light duty). Being behind the lines "for a rest," as the higher ranks facetiously put it, he had "clicked" this job from a tolerant S.M.

"There's a rumour I've just heard," I began, but Micky interrupted me.

"Yes, I've heard all about it; the G.O.C.'s (General Officer Commanding) coming round on an inspection," he said, "why the ruddy hell don't you come in with some *good* news?"

I could find no answer to cope with this question, except to assure Micky that I'd willingly be the bearer of good news if there were any floating about. I sat down on a pile of blankets and became interested in Micky's unique methods of working. It was worth watching to see him carefully sweeping little heaps of dust into minute holes with the aid of another chap's boot brush. This done, he wiped his hands on a towel, the virgin whiteness of which proclaimed the fact that it was not Micky's property. Micky is a philosopher of a cheery disposition, a fact which sometimes I have no appreciated, as for instance, when on one particularly wet and miserable morning he awoke me from my slumbers by dancing on my outstretched legs singing the while, "Hail! Smiling Morn—Smiling Morn!" He has also a very inventive and original mind, but these latter qualities I will speak more of anon.

It was about two hours later as we were having our tea in the seclusion of our bivvies, that the G.O.C., with his staff, came along. He was a resplendant vision in khaki, red and brown, with many hued ribbons across his breast. "Sit down, sit down," he said, as we all sprung to "shun" in acknowledgment of his greatness. With a cold dispassionate eye he inspected our lines, and, as the group moved on, we could hear him say, "Hum—yes, very creditable." We saw him stop at Micky's bivvy, which was just next but one to our own, and the satellites of the Great One stopped also. Micky's aforementioned inventive genius had led him to carve and erect a small notice board in the shape of a hand with the index finger pointing at the entrance to the "bivvy." On this proof of his artistic genius he had chalked the mystic word, "MYOBB." It was at this same board that the general's gaze was directed, and we waited for the inevitable question. Micky was standing at "attention" with an uncomfortable look on his usually smiling cherubic countenance, and it was to him the general turned, as he said, "Ah! I see, name of the bivouac—eh? but what does 'Myobb' mean." Micky answered not, and, no doubt, aware that there were numerous other eyes directed at him beside the general's, some with just cold curiosity depicted in them, and others (among which were my own) were full of ap-

"MIND YER OWN —— BUSINESS."

prehension. "Come, speak up, my lad," said the general, with an encouraging smile directed at Micky.

"Well, sir, I hardly like to tell you," said Micky in a rather hoarse voice.

"Oh, but we must know," replied the impatient general, "we must know what the word means."

You cannot ignore a command from an officer, and when that command comes from a brass-hatted, red-tabbed and much beribboned general, it is futile to try and find a way of evading the command. So Micky, evidently having reasoned somewhat thusly, cleared his throat and, with an almost despairing look on his face, stammered, "Well, sir, Myobb means—er—Mind Your Own bl—bl—Blinking Bizness!"

I recovered just in time to hear a deep laugh, and to see the group turning the corner of the line. But ever after that I had a great opinion of Micky, especially in the way he dealt with that adjective.

B.S.A BICYCLES

THERE'S always one safe course when selecting a new bicycle—see that it carries the B.S.A. name and the famous "Three Guns" trade mark shown below; they are a guarantee of highest quality material and workmanship.

B.S.A. Catalogue Free on request.

THE BIRMINGHAM SMALL ARMS COMPANY LIMITED, Small Heath, BIRMINGHAM

IN YOUR PARCEL

Just write "top-hole" across this advertisement, cut it out and send it to the Dad or Mater, the Girl or any of the folks at home as a gentle hint for your next parcel. Your parcel is not complete without Clarnico Lily Caramels—those delicious toothsome dainties made of cream, sugar, and almonds coated with chocolate. There's sheer joy in every bite.

Clarnico Lily Caramels are made by Clarke, Nickolls and Coomb's, Ltd., of London, and are obtainable at all good confectioners.

Clarnico Lily Caramels

Note Name and Address

ALLEN & WRIGHT,

Makers of High-Class Briar Pipes,

217, Piccadilly, W. | 39, St. Mary Axe, } E.C.
26, Poultry, E.C. | 7, King Street,

THE **A S** BRIAR
ACTIVE   SERVICE

Rich dark-Briar with Hand Finished Vulcanite Push Mouthpiece

4/6
Postage 6d

Extra Fine Quality with *Hand-Cut* Vul. M'thpiece **6/6**

EQUAL IN EVERY RESPECT TO PIPES SOLD AT MUCH HIGHER PRICES

NEW OILSKIN POUCHES.
Very light, strong, waterproof, keeps tobacco better than rubber.
To hold—2-3 ozs. **3/6**
Post free.

VELVET CALF CIGARETTE CASES.
To hold about 32, with space for Photo—**7/6**. Postage—6d.

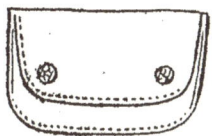
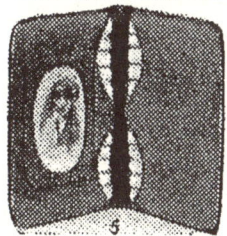

THIS IS THE CREAM

That makes all the difference to a Man's appearance.

ANZORA is the original Cream made by the original cream Manufacturers with 2 Gold Medals for First Quality plus 21 years—
EXPERIENCE

ANZORA is the non-greasy Hair Cream used by every common-sense, Military, Professional and Business Man who knows the value of personal appearance. Who realizes that "Tidy" Hair makes all the difference. If your scalp is dry use Anzora Viola which contains a little Anzora Oil of Violets. These quality preparations are sold by all Chemists, Hairdressers and Canteens. Sold in 1/6 and 2/6 double quantity bottles.

ANZORA PERFUMERY CO.
28, 32, 34, Willesden Lane, London, N.W. 6.

LITTLE BILLY AND THE MOUSE.

Army life appeared to be as bewildering to Private Binks as the pageantry of city life to a bushman. He had chawbacon written all over him, and soon became the butt of the camp. He never retaliated on his tormentors; he just writhed. He never betrayed symptoms of choler, though, occasionally, the wraith of pain flitted across his deep-set blue eyes. The best in him and the worst in him rarely became vocal. Hence he was dubbed the mouse, in spite of the fact that, physically, he was a Colossus.

The mouse was being unmercifully ragged one night when little Billy arrived on the scene. Unexpectedly Little Billy created a diversion.

His thin, little frame was shaking tremulously.

"It's a damn shame," he spluttered, "damn caddish, I call it, for the lot of you to attack one poor devil who hasn't the gift of retaliation, and it's damn bad taste."

A politician might have been more sonorous, but he certainly would not have proved so effective.

The crowd melted away. Many of the men cast sheepish glances at Little Billy as they moved off, for this feeble-looking little man had, by some mysterious means, won the respect of the whole camp. He was no soldier. Often that had been said of him, but there was something indefinable about him that made men careful of their language in his presence; he might have been a girl, so scrupulous were they in keeping a guard on their tongues.

Yet, as the men acknowledged, he was no prig. Indeed, as it had been put once, he was a pious man without the patents of piety. He was of all men most miserable when he had to attend church parade.

Little Billy, in short, was a bundle of paradoxes, and had that rare thing—personality.

After his protest the mouse was left in peace, though it must be confessed, there was no disposition to fraternise with him.

Little Billy, who in pre-war days had been a black-and-white artist, alone could "draw" him—I don't mean in the professional sense.

"He's lived in Guernsey," he told the others, "and can patter in French better than in English. He's quite a decent sort, really."

The Philistines, however, continued to keep the barrier up against the mouse.

With the winter Little Billy "put on years."

Coast defence work is no soft job when violent storms spend themselves against the cheerless dunes. The strongest suffered, and Little Billy was not too robust.

The unceasing guards and patrols, interspersed with periods of manual labour on the defences, wrought on him severely. He seemed to shrivel up, and his eyes lost their lustre.

One night he was on sentry duty, his post being outside a ramshackle shanty facing the sea. Within, his companions on guard slumbered fitfully. The interior was filthy; an oil lamp was the only illuminant.

Little Billy, coat collar up, shook and shivered. At times he almost felt like swooning. He was getting near the end of his tether.

"Oh," he muttered to himself, "I'll never stick it out. I must have an hour to go yet." His eyes closed for a moment, and he swayed a little. On the waste of waters before him lights on tossing ships at anchor blinked and bobbed.

He walked up and down a little. His feet were like lead. The sand under foot seemed to drag at them, and whirling sheets of sand stung his eyes. Waves of weakness surged through him. He began to rave a little, and to picture himself as the outstanding figure in a court martial should nature overcome him. He never even thought of calling on one of his fellows to relieve him. It wasn't done. His thoughts gradually resolved themselves into a confused jumble.

Again and again he tried to shake off sleep, but it returned again and again with relentless persistence.

Suddenly the roar of the sea subsided into a faint echo, soothing as a chant at evening's close, and Little Billy sank into oblivion.

It was with a shock he awoke. He was on his knees, his rifle on the sand beside him, with bayonet fixed. He scrambled to his feet hurriedly, though aching in every limb, seized the rifle as he rose, and came on guard.

Instinctively he had done the correct thing. He descried a figure approaching, and heard the word "friend."

"Advance, friend, and be recognised," cried Little Billy.

The figure advanced. It was visiting rounds.

"Pass, friend; all's well," said Little Billy, lowering his bayonet.

The officer chuckled. "That's the way to challenge," he said. "Your challenge absolutely shook me up. Everything all right?"

Little Billy blinked his mystification, but had sense enough to say everything was all right.

The officer disappeared within the shanty, reappearing a few moments later.

Then the mouse emerged with the corporal of the guard. The mouse was Little Billy's relief.

"Try and get a good sleep," said the mouse to Little Billy. "You'll be all the better for it." His voice was harsh, but quiet.

Little Billy entered the shanty, pondering, with wrinkled brows. He was very wide awake now. He issued forth again presently, and touched the mouse on the arm.

"Thanks, old boy," he said. "I'd never have seen him. I was damn near asleep."

"Yes, damn near," grunted the mouse, "Damn near." And he chuckled hoarsely.

HARRY BAXTER.

Bluejacket (who has been bowled for 0): "I KNEW WHAT WOULD 'APPEN IF I PUT THESE BLITHERING TORPEDO NETS ON." *Chas. Grave.*

OMAR REDIVIVUS.

I've just returned from Paradise, in need
Of opportunity to try the weed
Men call tobacco, and I'll say at once
My birth was too soon, much too soon, Indeed.

A book of verse underneath the bough,
A jug of wine is still all right, but now
A pipe is needed to complete the bliss,
I'll not return to Paradise, I vow.

And that adapted bowl men call a pipe,
Especially if its flavour's rich and ripe.
Lift not thy hand to do it scathe, or I
Will quickly have thee in a frenzied gripe.

And now I must return unto the skies,
And never more be seen by mortal eyes.
I must away, but yet, before I go,
I'll get a stock to take to Paradise.

Sapper H. N. SYMES.

Irate Old Gentleman (who has been kept waiting): "DOES THE WORKING OF THE LIFT INTERFERE WITH YOUR READING, MY LAD?"
Lift Boy: "NOT VERY MUCH, SIR."

Lt. E. Savereux, East Surreys.

Tommy: "— ? ! ? * * ! ! —" (*Deleted by Censor.*)

Pte. V. F. Cottrell, 112th Field Amb.

A REAR RANK PRIVATE

I don't go much on singing,
 And I sling an awful fist,
And I know as much of poetry
 As a bulldog does of whist,
But I'll try and tell a story
 If you think that that will do,
It's a mighty funny story,
 But I'll guarantee it's true.
There's no medals to his honour,
 Just a wooden cross instead,
For he's marching with the heroes
 In the vanguard of the dead.

He was just a rear rank private,
 With a private's tendencies
For standing at attention
 When he should have been at ease;
And he wasn't much to look at
 From the ladies' point of view,
But for getting into trouble,
 Or a most ungodly stew
I have never seen his equal
 Tho' I sail the seven seas,
Trouble rode upon his shoulders
 Like some grim and dread disease.

We were making eighteen hard miles,
 And the burning sun of June
Had our brains damn well nigh frazzled
 As we bivouaced at noon.
The chuck wasn't over plenty,
 Not enough to do you harm.
Just a hunk of bread and bully
 With a half-a-pint of warm.
I didn't feel like eating—
 Well, in fact, I had a head:
When your skin is full of vin rouge
 You don't hanker much for bread.

There are lots of men whose rations
 Leave a hole where they should fill,
So I looked around for someone
 And I spotted this guy Bill.
I could see he was a new one,
 Just out with the latest draft,
And between the chuck and marching
 He was finding it hard graft.
So I kinda grinned and beckoned,
 As I handed out the chuck,
He took it kinda gingerly,
 As though he couldn't trust his luck.

Have you seen a cur dog limping
 Thro' this world of kicks and cries,
With a wealth of love still burning
 In his great big dreamy eyes?
Have you felt his rough tongue licking
 As you touched his poor lean flanks?
Have you seen his stub tail wagging
 Out his great and heartfelt thanks?
Then you'll understand my meaning
 When I tell you, and the way
I came to meet this hero
 On that hell-hot summer's day.

As we formed fours and marched off,
 There was "Old Bill" by my side,
You could see he meant to stick it, too.
 For he smiled at every stride.
Well, I found it kinda pleasant
 As my ears began to hum
And the dust clouds well nigh chocked me,
 And a dirty kinda scum
Seemed to wipe out all the universe
 And blended land and trees,
As he took my pack and rifle
 And carried both with ease.

I was pretty tired on starting,
 And before the day was o'er
The bread I'd cast on waters
 Multiplied ten times and more.
I shared the grub, he shared the weight,
 And ever from that day
He showed his fine devotion
 In his great big clumsy way.
He was like a child when sober,
 Just as innocent of guile,
And you couldn't help but like him
 When once you saw him smile.

In his cups he was a devil,
 Just a howling, crazy loon,
Like a maniac who has his spells
 At the fulness of the moon.
I could always get him quieted
 When he had too much to drink,
And we always bunked together
 When he wasn't in the clink—
Which, to tell the truth, was seldom,
 For he used to like to play
At beating up the "copp'rs"
 In a friendly sort of way.

Then the night (I'll not forget it
 If I live a thousand years),
We were lying in a shell hole,
 Showing nothing but our ears;
Showing nothing, only listening—
 That might sound quite soft to you,
But the job that sounds quite easy
 Is the hardest one to do.
There was very little doing,
 For the night was like a tomb,
'Cept when now and then a flare light
 Helped to intensify the gloom.

I remembered winter evenings
 Round the cosy kitchen fire,
When the wind moaned down the chimney
 And the cheery flame leaped higher;
How I coaxed and teased till mother
 Told me tales of ghosts and spooks,
Till my hair displaced my bonnet
 And my little frame just shook.
Such a feeling now possessed me,
 And in every post and tree
I could see a grim face outlined
 Every shade an enemy.

Then a clammy hand descended
 And gripped my windpipe tight,
And in that moment all my fears,
 Yes, every trace of fright
Had vanished like a shadow,
 As when sunshine melts the snow,
And I struggled like a maniac
 But, alas, it was no go.
Yet I struggled all the harder,
 Yes, I fought like hell until
I could see we were surrounded,
 Then I thought, "Oh, where is Bill?"

This must have been the fear then
 That gripped me as I lay,
'Twasn't all imagination,
 But a "hunch" as clear as day,
And I cussed my dam-fool fancies
 As I squirmed beneath the foe,
And I swore if I was taken
 There'd be one Hun less to go.
Then out from the black shadows
 Loomed a shadow blacker still,
And I heaved a sigh of welcome
 As I recognised Old Bill.

Have you seen the lightning flashing
 'Cross the peaceful evening sky?
Have you seen the grey hawk swooping
 On his victim from on high?
Have you seen the clean, proud boxer
 As he crouches for a spring?
Have you seen his strong lithe arms
 Shoot out with vicious swing?
Have you seen the patient tabby
 With her sleek and sleepy eyes?
Have you seen her tiny victim
 As she hits him by surprise?

That's the way Bill made his entrée,
 And the fellow that gripped me
Found a bayonet in his midrif
 Where his supper ought to be.
Then commenced a damn fine shindy,
 Not a sound disturbed the night,
It was cold steel and not bullets,
 It was death, grim death, that fight.
They'd advantage in the numbers,
 We were two, they now were eight,
But with a little fancy-stick work
 We could make that item straight.

As before I cursed the darkness,
 Now I blessed it all the more,
For it mystified the enemy,
 And sort of evened up the score.
So out we leaped together,
 Two short grunts were our reward,
As we lunged, then jabbed, then parried,
 Right about and up on guard.
Once again we leapt together,
 With our bayonets slightly lower,
As we swung back in position
 The score stood two to four.

As we steadied down to business
 Old Bill laughed out soft and low,
"'Cheero! me old side kicker,
 We're five up and four to go."
Now the foeman changed his tactics,
 And they rushed us all around,
But I brought one upright standing
 As I pinned him to the ground.
I was now without a rifle,
 So I jumped to get a stray,
But a German stood before me,
 And his bayonet barred the way.

Did you ever see a rattler
 When just about to strike?
Did he hold you kind of speechless,
 Sort of fascinated like?
That's the way that German held me
 As I watched his slightest stir,
He had no heart for fighting,
 I could see he was a cur.
I watched him draw the rifle,
 But before the point was made,
Like a flash Bill jumped to save me,
 And lit square upon the blade.

When I'd finished with the German
 I lifted "Old Bill's" head,
As I held him in my arms
 I could see that he was dead.
Well, I acted kind of childish then,
 For a man with all my years,
But I felt a whole lot better
 When I wiped away the tears.
Then among the ghostly shadows,
 Broken-hearted at my loss,
I hollowed out a shallow grave,
 And I raised a tiny cross.

As a big gun in the distance
 Boomed out his funeral knell,
I knelt a moment by his side
 And said my last farewell.
With the foemen dead around him
 Where his feet last pressed the sod,
In a ground-sheet close I wound him,
 And I left his soul to God.
There's no medals to his honour,
 Just a wooden cross instead,
But he's marching with the heroes
 In the vanguard of the dead.

Pte. M. J. J. SULLIVAN.

Sentry: "HERE! YOU THERE!"   Rustic: "WHA-A-A-T?"
Sentry: "GOT A BIT O' BACCY, MATE?"   Rustic: "NO—I ARN'T."
Sentry: "WELL THEN, GET OUT O' THIS FIELD."

H. Mallalieu.

Officer (after lecture): "NOW, ARE THERE ANY QUESTIONS YOU WOULD LIKE TO ASK ON THE SUBJECT?"
Pte. Foozle: "DO YOU THINK WE ARE WINNING, SIR?"

Pte. H. Greenhalgh, 1/12th North Lancs. Rgt.

THE FOOD CONTROL.

"NOT A BAD DINNER THAT FOR THREE AND SIXPENCE, EH, JACK?"
"FIRST RATE, UNCLE BOB—LET'S GO SOMEWHERE ELSE AND HAVE ANOTHER."
Pioneer H. A. Lewis, R.E.

AN "AFFAIRE" OF ARTILLERY.

The opinion of the battery is that Gunner Percy Popple has only one weakness—he will talk shop. Having been Percy's best pal since he joined the Umpteenth battery, I am in a position to state, without being accused of getting my dentures in Percy's back, that he has another fault equally bad. I refer to his susceptibility to the charms of the opposite sex.

He can tell you exactly how many wheels are in the 18-pr. Q.F. gun, and with equal facility he will inform you the standard age of the flapper in any of the last ten years, and why so many married women wear feathers in their hats. In three minutes he can dash off a fifty-word letter to a girl friend in Blighty that will produce a parcel of eatables by return post, and in the same space of time he can find the angle of sight at a given range and given contours.

Recently we took up a couche position after a seven months' sojourn in the wilderness. We came into action at a farm, sharing the buildings with the fermier and fermière, and setting our aiming-posts in the green corn beyond the garden. The boys donned white lanyards, "dug out" and blackened their boots, and chased the verdigrease from their buttons with "Soldiers' Friend." Then they proceeded to get acquainted with the many estaminets and coffee-shops in the vicinity, and the mesdames and mam'selles therein.

Percy was in his element. He gave his lanyard two coats of blanco one evening, polished his chin-strap, and substituted shiny new brass buttons for the "grey-back" variety on his smoke-helmet bag.

"Don't ask questions," he said, when he saw my knowing smile. "I'll make a clean breast of it. It's the coffee-shop down the road. Her name's Jeanne; she's fair and plump, and somewhere about deece-nuff ans, I should say."

"Perce," I addressed him paternally, "you're too sudden. You'll never make a conquest. The last time you went a-wooing was when we were out at rest in December. You want time to practice, kid, before you attempt conquests. How can you talk sweet nothings all at once when you've been spouting elevation and deflection and degrees and minutes for seven months? You're premature, my son; you'll only give a good position away."

"Level your bubble," replied Percy, in his usual peculiar patois. "This is where I put my knowledge of gunnery to good use, old boy. I came into action last night at the coffee-shop, and registered my zone to a nicety. I've laid a zero-line on that damsel's heart, and I'll get a direct hit there before long. I put up a practise barrage with all the French I know, and the signs were encouraging."

Lest he should carry his analogy to the point of boredom, I hastily stood aside and let him proceed.

He came into the gun-pit a couple of hours later, with (as he might have said himself) "several degrees depression on."

"Poor shooting," I observed. "Check your range and angles."

"Angles are all right," retorted Percy. "Don't know why I failed. She only changed her position once; when I was getting warm on the zero line—chaffing in pidgin-French, you know. She got talking to another chap, an M.M.P. wallah. I put on a big angle to get at her—talked to the copper myself. And, would you credit it, she changed her position again, went back to frying eggs, while the M.P. bored me stiff talking about barmaids. You see, she came right back on the original position, plump on the zero line, and me with an extreme left switch on!"

"Very much left," I commented. "And then you stood easy? So much for the impregnable Fort Jeanne."

But Percy is persistent. He made another attempt on the following evening, and this time was completely repulsed by hard and direct counter-battery work from the lady's eyes. That was all I could elicit from him in the way of official intelligence. During the following day I called at the coffee-shop myself, and indulged in coffee, eggs, bread and butter—and a good look at the fair Jeanne. It was she who ventured upon conversation when I ordered a second brace of "oofs."

"Bon," said she. "Bully beef no bon."

"Too many oofs no bon," I deposed, trying to sound discouraging.

"Mais oui," she protested. "William eat four œufs often. Him big, strong. Charlee, sometimes six. Him, too, strong. Some men say, 'Deux œufs, deux œufs,' all ze time. Them petit, no bon."

I had a shrewd suspicion that the six sous given in exchange for each egg had much to do with Jeane's enthusiasm for the "oof" as nourishment for the English soldier. However, I didn't say so to Percy. I reported the skirmish, and advised him of my deductions.

"That girl, Percy, measures a man's worth by his gastronomic abilities. You want to eat eggs, Percy, my boy, eggs, eggs—and always more eggs. Now I've given you the secret. Battery, action. Go in and win."

"By this time," said Percy despondently, "you ought to know that three eggs, boiled or fried, are my limit. I'll have to limber up and retire. Ah, well, she was getting distant—almost out of range, in fact."

"Sour grapes!" I mixed the metaphor shamelessly. "It's sheer incompetence that's been your undoing, Percy. You can't load up the ammunition quickly enough. There's only one solution to the ammunition question."

"And that is?"

"Ask Lloyd George. Ask the 'Daily Mail.' You are dense, Perce. How did we solve the greatest problem of the war?"

Percy cogitated profoundly. Genius always springs its surprises tersely.

"Shells," said I and nothing more.

"But I don't see—shells?—how?——"

"Listen. I've reconnoitred a new position for you, Percy. The correct time to come into action is about the seventh hour of the evening, less fifteen minutes, when Madame will serve you, and Jeanne will be absent, as is her habit, for the evening meal. And, madame, as is her reprehensible habit, will leave the remains of many suppers on the table where you sit. On the stroke of seven, exit Madame, enter Jeanne. You, meanwhile, have gathered on to your plate the shells of the dear—very dear—departed 'oofs' left by previous patrons. When mam'selle——"

Percy placed one hand over my mouth, and very soberly gave me the other to grasp.

"I hope you get that commish before the ranks dull your intellect," said he. "You ought to be on the staff. I'll come into action to-night at 6.45 prompt, divisional time."

You will be pleased to learn that my amorous comrade made several direct and most effective hits that evening. On the authority of the best observers I have it that he enabled all arms to make a very successful encircling movement.

"You were right," he told me later. "The secret is 'shells.' But I must make sure of a continuous supply. How many eggs can you consume at one sitting?"

"Four, as a rule," I answered, modestly. "Six when I skip tea in the battery."

"Bon! You come with me, and I'll treat you to supper every evening, sonny. I should always have at least six shells when she appears. You can make the total eight when other customers are few, or when rivals are about at the critical hour."

"I see. I am going to be a sort of shell factory."

"Not at all! You're being appointed Minister of Munitions."

As William and Charlie of the big appetites are only unconscious rivals to Percy, I am sanguine of holding my portfolio till next "pay-out."

BREECH-BLOCK.

ONE OF OUR FRIENDS.

The following letter reaches us from Mesopotamia, addressed "Blighty Office":—"Will you please supply me with the blighty papers, it rather amuse me with the contents that into it. I was sick in hospital, and can get no rest during the day, and a kind friend of mine give me a blithy to read their. I managed to rest a bit. I don't know wheather you will admit it to me. Don't fail to send them every week if possible help and also the daily mirror. Guess that will keep me up for a while; am only taking a chance because I have never done anything such as that and I see what I can do for you. Enclose please send me the proper address."

EVE OF BATTLE.

You sleep so quietly! Who at dawn must go
Into the mouth of hell. The stage is set
For a new tragedy of blood; and yet
You lie like tired children here below
These shattered trees; and your young faces show
No marks of fear! You dream, smile, and forget
The horrors you have seen, death whom you met
So lately, and must face again to-morrow.

Sleep on! You shall not fight the worse, perchance,
Because your last were happy dreams of home.
Smile! For death is already half o'ercome
When challenged by youth's gay and fearless glance.
And near to an unending rest are some
Of you; so soon cometh deliverance.

G. A. R. GROVES.

Overheard on destroyer's bridge at sea.

Lookout (H.O.) to officer of watch reports:

"Vessel on starboard bow, sir!"

O. of W. (putting glasses to his eyes): "I cannot see anything; just point it out to me."

L. O. (fed up, and just noticing the rising moon): "Why, on the starboard side of the moon, sir."

A. G. REED.

ARGUMENT!

FATHER: "I tell you this man you want to marry won't be able to keep you in shoe leather!"
DAUGHTER: "But I hardly ever need new boots or shoes, Dad. I make mine last just twice as long, and retain their smartness to the end now that I use CHERRY BLOSSOM BOOT POLISH!"

Tins of all dealers in Black, Brown, and Tonette.

TONETTE *is the dark stain polish which imparts the correct colour to Sam Browne Belts and all tan leather military equipments.*

9D. EACH. TARGET 9D. EACH.

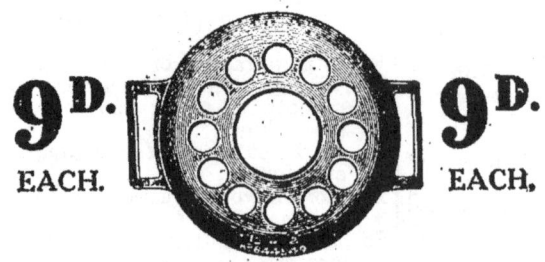

WRIST WATCH PROTECTOR.

Incomparable in Quality, Attractiveness, Finish.

Nickel Plated, and warranted to wear white throughout.

FITS ALL TYPES AND SIZES OF WRIST WATCHES.

JOHN WARRILLOW, LTD., Hampton House, BIRMINGHAM.

Buy your Gramophone Records at Aeolian Hall

WITH the introduction to the public of the now famous "Aeolian Vocalion," the tone-perfect gramophone, we recently opened magnificent new premises devoted to the sale of gramophones and records, and designed to provide facilities and conveniences offered previously by no other establishment.

Aeolian Hall is the most convenient and comfortable place in London at which to make a selection of records. The Record Department is equipped to hold a stock of 10,000 records at one time; it is furnished with a suit of sound-proof rooms in which records may be tried before purchase, and it is conducted by an experienced staff whose advice and assistance are placed unreservedly at your service. Whilst you pay no more for your records, you obtain advantages that no other retail establishment can offer.

You are invited to hear the latest Columbia successes at Aeolian Hall. If unable to call, ask to be placed upon our Catalogue Mailing List, which will insure regular advice of the current selections as issued.

THE AEOLIAN CO., Ltd.

(FORMERLY THE ORCHESTRELLE CO.),

 **Aeolian Hall,**
131-137, NEW BOND ST., LONDON, W.1.

Direct from Factory TO Soldier at the Fronts

BY POST.

Order Z	280 Wills'	"WILD WOODBINE"	Cigarettes	4/-
Order V	230 Wills'	"GOLD FLAKE"	Cigarettes	5/-
Order T	500 Player's	"NAVY CUT"	Cigarettes	10/-
Order U	1000 Wills'	"WILD WOODBINE"	Cigarettes	11/9
Order Q	450 Wills'	"THREE CASTLES"	Cigarettes	10/6
Order P	1000 Wills'	"GOLD FLAKE"	Cigarettes	18/-
Order O	1000 Player's	"NAVY CUT"	Cigarettes	19/-

CANNOT ACCEPT ORDERS FOR SMALLER QUANTITIES THAN ABOVE.

Above Prices Include Postage Which Ensures Quick Despatch.

Orders may be handed to any Tobacconist OR POSTED DIRECT TO

BRITISH-AMERICAN TOBACCO CO., LTD.,
(Ex. Dept.) Westminster House, No. 7, Millbank, London, S.W.

Near the trenches

it is difficult to always get the necessaries one requires, so if you can't get T.M. at your canteen, ask your friends to send a supply in each parcel. T.M. is the preparation which will remove "tongue bite" in addition to keeping one's teeth white and mouth sweet.

T.M. The Standard DENTIFRICE for Everybody.

Powder, 6d. Tins. Paste, 1/- Tubes.

Of Canteens or Chemists, or CHRISTY's, (B), Old Swan Lane, E.C.4.

THE END IN SIGHT.

"LOOK, HUGHIE,—IT'S ONLY A HUNNER MILES TO BERLIN."
"TUTS MAN, WULLIE! THAT WAS AFORE THE WAR. AFTER A' THIS ADVANCING, IT CANNA BE SAE FAR NOO."
Sergt. W. Sawers, R.A.M.C.

TOMMY'S FAREWELL TO HIS FRIEND.

By JOSEPH MEANEY.

Well, Basil, old fellow, faithful little chum, the end has come, and I have said my last good-bye to you. To-night, for the first time since the day you made me your friend, you are not by my side. To-morrow the "Tommies" who got to know and like you, because of your silent devotion to me, will say, "Where's old Basil?" and I shall have to tell them that you have gone out of my life, although you will live in my memory—always.

I found it very hard saying "good-bye" to you this afternoon, Basil, old boy. Three times I came back after I had said "farewell" because I found it so hard to leave you. You looked at me very strangely, Basil, each time I turned to go. Those big, sad eyes of yours looked after me and drew me back. Each time I came back the light of happiness shone in those eyes—it was always there when you were by my side, Basil! When I took hold of your paw and stroked your head for the last time and said "Good-bye, Basil, my little chum," a big lump rose in my throat—it was very hard saying good-bye to you, Basil!

You were very fond of me, Basil, and you never forgot the little service I did for you when I found you lying helpless and friendless by the side of the Somme. I nursed you through your illness, and made you warm and comfortable by the cook's fire. You were grateful, Basil, for this little kindness, and all through these long, lonely months I have had your affection—the biggest thing you had to give. We have had some rough times together, Basil, old boy, but you've stuck to me. You've followed me through the mud and rain when your poor old limbs have been racked with rheumatism. And then, when I've made you comfortable at night in the corner of the old barn, you've slipped quietly out and taken up your place against the door where the cold draught came through. You were "guarding" me, Basil, old boy, looking after your friend. It was just your little way of showing your gratitude, but you were wearing yourself out.

How happy you were when we set out for that little stroll across the fields each evening. It pleased me to see you tumbling over in the grass, and, foolishly, trying to catch your little stumpy tail between your teeth. I used to call you an old fool and tell you you were old enough to know better, but it made me laugh, and I think that was the reason you played the fool so much. You often amused my companions by your little silly tricks, and I know they will miss you. A few weeks ago they made you a "Sergeant," Basil. They thought it would please me. It did! and I was happy when I put your new disc on the little collar I made for you. The collar and disc are in my pocket now, and I shall carry them with me to England, where I had hoped to take you, Basil, so that you might live out the days which I thought remained to you—in comfort.

I shall never forget the last time we were out together, Basil. You were trotting along behind me, when a car came along. I thought it would clear you all right, Basil, but you were almost blind, and ran into it. I picked you up, poor old fellow, and you ceased moaning. The motorists asked how far I was going, and when I told them they said "You've got a long walk"—and went off. It wouldn't have taken their car very long at the rate it was going when they went over you, Basil!

To-night, as I sit writing this little farewell to you, Basil, faithful and and devoted chum of a "Tommy" in France, the hot tears are running down my cheeks. These tears are tears of sorrow for you, Basil, my little pal, because I know how much I shall miss your fond old head resting affectionately on my knee, and those big sad, and almost sightless, eyes of yours looking up into my face. I shall miss you when I go on that little stroll across the fields—alone. I used to talk to you about Blighty, and the friends at home who mentioned you in their letters. And you often spoke to me, Basil, old fellow, and although I didn't understand your language I always knew what you meant.

Good-bye, Basil. Fond and faithful little pal—farewell. The days that remain will seem very long and very lonely without you, Basil, old fellow. My heart is very heavy to-night, Basil —the first night you are not by my side. Dear little chum—good-bye!

MEN WE SELDOM MEET.

"JULES."

In a certain French seaport, to which the gentle Hun pays frequent visits by air, the powers that be have decreed, rightly or wrongly, that warning of impending danger should be given. Thus, at frequent intervals, night is made hideous by the sounds of foghorns, whistles, and syrens.

These sounds, I may add, are far more hideous and nerve-racking than the tearing crashes of falling bombs or the ominous thrum of the raiders' motors.

These machines for the emission of hideous noises have to be operated by human agency, and so far the employment bureaus have not been overwhelmed with applicants

Generally, soldiers, unfit for more arduous duties at the front, are employed, but there is one exception, Jules. That's not his name, of course, but it will do.

An old lightship, with foghorn (the most efficient emitter of hideousness of all), has been pressed into service. Her foghorn has been nicknamed "Mournful Mary," which is quite a misnomer. It should be "Roaring Roger," or "Raging Reggie," except that a ship being feminine, I suppose "Angry Annie" would be more correct. At any rate her emissions are anything but mournful. Fancy saying 10,000 Bulls of Bashan, roaring all together, sounded mournful.

In normal times she counted amongst her crew an old man, Jules, and for years he has operated the sound emitter for the benefit of sailors, and he has learned to love it. So much so that during the two and a half years that it has been used as a warning he has continued to operate it.

Of course he is as safe as houses.

By the way, have you ever seen a house which has been hit by an aerial torpedo or a 12-inch H.E. shell? Yes?

To-day, however, he is the proudest man in all France, for a wise and just government has ordered that he be decorated for "consistent courage and devotion to duty under most trying conditions during a period of two years and eight months," and this very day the Croix de Guerre was pinned on his breast by the General Commanding the district.

Jules is only seventy-eight, and a conscientious objector —to the Hun.

All this I learned to-night during a raid.

I love the sound of "Mournful Mary," or "Angry Annie"—call it what you will.

Lt. B. W. GLUCKSTEN.

1.—THE MAN WHO STICKS TO THE PHRASE-BOOK TILL HE REALLY "SPOKE LIKE A NATIVE."

2.—THE CONSCIENTIOUS LEADSWINGER WHO REFUSES HIS PAY WHENEVER HE THINKS HE HAS NOT EARNED IT.

3.—THE M.T. DRIVER WHO WAS CAUGHT DRIVING WITHIN THE SPEED LIMIT.

Pte. A. E. Bestall, A.S.C.

TO AN OLD FLAME.

Oft in the silence of the evening's rest,
Comes to my questioning eyes a vision fair,
The fine artistic line of one sweet breast,
The rounded curves of one dear form, the rare
Perfection of my love, before whose shrine
I burnt much incense in gay yuletide ways;
Oh! that I could for one short hour eclipse
The horrid squalor of these latter days,
Once more gaze on that loveliness so fine,
Call all that bounteous feast of splendour mine,
And draw that honeyed fragrance to my lips.

How fresh the memory of the day we met,
Still I can see your hat of berried leaves,
The sweet aroma clinging round you yet
Stays in the tangle that remembrance weaves.
Desire was raised in me that could not fail,
Though I was then of but a tender age.
(You wore some charms of silver next your heart),
Nothing could still my all-consuming rage
For possession. I found you soft and frail,
Yielding before the onrush of the male;
Then for a lonely year we were apart.

Did later manhood teach me to restrain
My hungry passion, or your charms beguile
My once uneasy conscience, though the pain
Of sure repentance followed in a while?
Yes, though, alas! the case was all too clear,
Temptation scarce was there before the fall.
You, wanton charmer, had me in your toils,
For never once you showed a trace of fear,
Nor made a struggle as drew you near,
Each year I came unto your siren's call.

It yet may chance that by the agency
Of some kind friend who of my weakness knows,
This Xmas we may meet and merrily
Speed a few moments as the red wine flows.
Then by performance of some reckless feat
Of hungry appetite, I yet may gain,
By ruined health, old Blighty's welcome shore,
Not for duration to come out again.
Then with what ardour shall I gladly greet
At home, yes, how contentedly I'll eat
You there, my Xmas plum pudding, once more.
                    Pte. G. A. GIBBS.

A QUARTER GROWL.

The quartermaster's face it wore a most emphatic frown,
He muttered and he spluttered and he eyed me up and down,
His stores were stocked like Liberty's with togs of every guise,
And I but craved one tunic, no matter what the size:
For lo! my upper ornament did green and mossy look,
The cloth was quite transparent, and the colour took its hook.
It was a splendid camouflage for any sort of ground,
But my eloquence proved futile 'gainst that atmosphere profound.
How I pleaded, how I wrangled, but my cries were all in vain,
For he never ceased his writing as he growled out, "Call again!"

Anon I sought the quarter's stores when leaves were turning sere,
My tunic, autumn-tinted and falling like the year.
I gazed around and noted all the uniforms so clean,
Those soft, warm, cosy tunics with their beauteous khaki sheen.
And I dreamt of gleaming buttons, polished boots and jaunty hat,
I'd even thoughts of swagger-canes, if pay would run to that;
But what I also noticed, and the sight my courage shook,
There sat the quarter writing in that never-ending book,
And to my anguished whisper came an answer that was plain,
As he spun round (business fashion) and growled, "What! you here again?"

Sergeant-Major (to man who has slipped): "HERE, WOT D'YOU MEAN SITTING IN THE MUD WHEN AN OFFICER APPROACHES? WHY DIDN'T YOU SALUTE? DIDN'T YOU SEE THE STARS?"
Culprit: "YESSIR, I SAW THE STARS—ONLY I COULDN'T COUNT 'EM, THEY WERE SO MANY, AND WERE ALL MIXED UP IN THE MUD." *Pte. J. Wood, 5th Army L'dy.*

I've mapped a little hades in the best Dantean style,
And if Nicky gets my notion I can quite afford to smile.
It's a cold Antarctic chamber full of draughts and ink and books,
And it's there for thin-clad quarters with pinched and frozen looks,
They'll be sitting writing, writing, through eternities of time,
With endless rows of paybooks each to balance to a dime.
They will draw their rags around them as they drop off thread by thread;
Should Nicky then appoint me there as departmental head,
Enthroned on bales of bright new togs I'd watch their shame and pain,
And to each chattering protest I would growl—"*Again? Again??*"
                    Pte. JOHN McSKIMMING.

"SOMEWHERE" IN "BLIGHTY."

There's a gap in the hedge where the sunbeams play,
And the breeze sweeps the Downs for a long, long way;
And I saw someone there, in the twilight dim,
With his new khaki sleeve round his girl so slim.
  "Laddie in khaki, lassie in blue,
    We have a place in our hearts for you.
  There we will keep you, there you shall stay,
    Making life brighter in love's sweet way."

Will you come to the gap in the hedge with me?
There is somebody there you would like to see,
And a welcome you'll find, I can well believe,
In your jacket of blue, with it's empty sleeve.
  "Soldier in khaki, soldier in blue,
    We have a prayer on our lips for you;
  Here in 'Old Blighty,' or far, far away,
    May God take care of you, day by day."
                    (per) GRACE MABERLEY-JORDAN.

Yokel (who unexpectedly finds himself laid low on menacing the Parson):
"ONLY YOUR CLOTH PROTECTS YOU."
Parson: "DOES IT? WELL, IT'S NOT GOING TO PROTECT *you!*"
D. W. and Lt. McCulloch, Canadians.

"GEORDIE, THE POCKET CONCERT."

It was Tiggle who first thought of it. He said: "How would it be if I were a lonely soldier?"

"A lonely stomach-ache," commented Jakes. "Why, you have more letters and parcels than all the rest of us put together."

"Yes, I know that," said Tiggle. "But how would it be if I was slowly pining away for a gramophone to entertain me brave but cheery chums?"

Neither Jakes nor Wardle seemed to grasp his idea. They both stared at him in perplexed fashion, and Pongelow said sarcastically:

"Well. 'Ow would it be? You could go on pining, couldn't you?"

"You haven't got me, Steve," sighed Tiggle. "You are the fat-headedest lot of blighters I ever struck in me natural. I mean, couldn't I write for one to one of those kind-hearted old gentlemen who make it a hobby to relieve the sufferings of our pore soldier-men?"

"Gee, that would do it, wouldn't it?" cried Jakes.

"Lumme! write straight away," said Pongelow. "We'll be back at Beauvillers in ten days with old mother Give-it-away. Blimey! What 'ave we all been thinking about?"

So Tiggle wrote, and the days dragged on, and the 9,001 Brigade Runners performed their arduous duties with more or less of that species of comment which earned for them the name of the Nine Thousand and First Grousers. Then the Brigade moved back into Beauvillers, and on the second evening a bulky case, "c/o Forwarding Officer," was handed in by the Transport.

"Don't make pigs of yourselves," said Transport, leering in at the doorway with acute misunderstanding of the contents of the box. A large piece of cheese-rind shrapnel rewarded his comments, and he fled into the night.

Then Geordie came out into the effulgent rays of five guttering candles. It was Pongelow who named it so, and he stroked the bright enamel of the instrument with something akin to affection.

"Eighteen blooming records," said Jakes.

HOME ON LEAVE.

"OUGHT I TO HAVE A SHAVE?"
F. S.

"And now the soulful soldiers, after the 'orrors of many an 'ard-fought field, can lie down and enjoy theirselves," said Pongelow, in bad imitation of Tiggle's florid style of speech.

With this announcement the Pocket Concert started on its career. When it had played eighteen records about eighteen times each, a wrathful sergeant put his head in at the door and glared balefully round the crowded apartment—for the sound of the music had attracted four cooks, five signallers, and about a score of the transport.

"The brigadier sends his compliments," said the sergeant sarcastically, "and he'd like to know if you'd play him 'Ome, Sweet 'Ome.'" Then, with a sudden change of tone, he added, "And as for you, you crooked legged mule-dusters, get orf to it."

The transport men knew the description only too well, and, sighing, left for their billets. Even Geordie had to stay his brazen voice at last, but not without sundry threats from the provost sergeant who came to see lights out.

The next day we had Geordie for breakfast, Geordie for dinner, Geordie for tea, and Geordie for supper, and in addition, Geordie in between whiles, for there was always some of us in the billet, and rarely more than three of us on duty at any one time.

Pongelow came in late. He had been to the 9,000 Brigade Headquarters for over two hours waiting for an answer, and was in a bad temper. Also Madame Give-it-away had charged him fifty centimes for two candles, which was typical of her generosity.

"Can't you get a few more records," he said petulantly, regarding Geordie who was "Marching Past" with the Guards with great enthusiasm. "I'm sick of that blessed toon. The only one with any guts in it is that 'Pig and Whistle trot.'"

"Poor Mr. Pongelow means the 'Fox trot,'" explained Tiggle. "It is all the same to his gallant but uneducated ear."

"Never mind my ear," said Pongelow, "take that record orf of it."

But Geordie anticipated his wishes by coming to the end of this disc, and I turned it over and started on the companion tune of "Waltz Me Around Again, Willie."

"Let's have 'Down Among the Dead Men' next," said Jakes, rummaging among the records on the floor.

"I'm goin' to 'ave the 'Pig and Whistle,'" vociferated Pongelow, also beginning to rummage.

"My favourite is 'Alice, Where Art Thou,'" said Bloomer, handing over this imperishable masterpiece.

The situation began to get warm, and I thought it prudent to vacate my post in favour of Wardle, who coaxed Geordie into playing "They Didn't Believe Me."

"And when I tell them, and I'm certainly going to tell them," sang Geordie, "that I'm the man whose——" Then he was rudely interrupted and the syncopated strains of the "Fox trot" broke the comparative silence.

This was too much for Jakes.

"I'm going to have the 'Dead Men,'" he shouted. He tore the whirling "Fox trot" from its platform and hurled it to the floor. "Take that and yer 'Pig and Whistle,'" he cried. But his triumph was short-lived. With one

Sandy: "LEND ME A FRANC, TAM."
Tam: "NA, I CANNA DAE THAT."
Sandy: "IT'S A SMA' THING TO REFUSE."
Tam: "AY, BUT YOU WOULDNAE PAY ME BACK, AND THEN YOU AN' ME WAD QUARREL; SO WE MAY JUST AS WEEL QUARREL NOO, WHILE THE MONEY'S IN MY POCKET."

Horace Gaffron.

sweep of his arm, Pongelow swept Jakes's choice from his hand and the two records mingled in waxy fragments on the floor.

Bloomer, too, hastening up with "Alice," was forestalled by Tiggle, who bore the immortal music of "Put Me Among the Girls," and Bloomer's quick revenge completed a toll of four records and eight items of Geordie's repertoire.

For a moment we all gazed thunderstruck.

"What's your favourite, Higgs?" asked Pongelow, breaking the spell.

"Waltz Me Around Again, Willie," I said innocently. Then, before any of us could interfere, a fifth record joined the wreckage.

Tiggle tittered. Three Jocks in a corner giggled. Pongelow laughed in triumph. Bloomer and Jakes laughed at Tiggle's titter, and then everybody broke into such a roar of laughter as had never been heard before in the billet of the 9,001st Grousers. Affrighted passers-by stayed in their tracks, the walls quivered and shook, three candles were blown out, and Madame Give-it-Away came in and said:

"Assez. Assez. Taissez-vous."

On the next day a terrible accident happened. Pongelow fancies himself as a juggler, and he was demonstrating his ability with two large bricks, to Geordie's accompaniment, when there occurred one of those miscalculations which even the greatest jugglers cannot always avoid. The ponderous bricks collided in mid-air, swerved a little, and then both together jumped straight upon the faithful Geordie with the crash of a bursting bomb.

We rushed frantically to the rescue, and picked up the injured Geordie from the cruel, hard floor with tender, loving care. We placed him on the table and made a fairly accurate, though inexpert, diagnosis of the wounds.

"The tympanum's bust," said Tiggle.

"So's the bloomin' horn," said Pongelow.

"And the motor won't wind up," added Wardle, tinkering with the machinery.

"Poor, poor old Geordie," lamented Tiggle. "No more will his sweet voice cheer and hearten the gallant troops."

And our visitors filed sadly out, leaving us to do the best we could with the invalid. But all efforts were unavailing until next morning, at breakfast, Tiggle announced that he had solved the difficulty.

He announced it cryptically, as usual. "Treacle," he said.

"What's treacle to do with it?" asked the reckless Pongelow, whose wild spirits were almost entirely subdued by remorse.

"We can mend the tympanum with treacle," explained Tiggle, and so roused us from the despair which Geordie's silence had pressed upon us. We crowded round, and Tiggle carefully patched up the injured part with a plaster composed of the piece of thin paper from a gold flake packet liberally smeared with golden syrup.

The effect was magical. A record was put upon the platform and Tiggle stirred it round with his finger, in place of the usual motive power. Imagine our joy and gratitude when a deep bass voice gave forth in slow and weird syllables the opening lines of "Come Into the Garden, Maud."

"It's a bit too slow," said Wardle, listening with the air of a connoisseur.

Tiggle stirred round more quickly, and the voice rose into a falsetto scream in a language which none of us could understand.

"That's too quick," said Pongelow. "The pore feller's supposed to be a tenor, not a threepenny bit."

So Tiggle moderated the pace and struck the happy medium, and thereafter, whenever we are in our precious billet at Madame Give-it-Away's, Geordie never lacks a faithful attendant to revolve him.

He is broken in the war, but he still manfully carries on, and our affection for our old pal, the Pocket Concert, is unbounded. Perhaps Geordie himself could not tell us how he feels about it all, but treacle certainly suits him.

And, up to the time of writing, the 9,001st Grousers have still nine unbroken records to feed him with.

Pte. F. FAWCETT.

CHRISTMAS PASS-TIMES.

By HENRY E. DUDENEY,
The King of Puzzle Makers.

AN EVENTFUL CHRISTMAS JOURNEY.

CARRYING THE BAGS.

On a Christmas journey that I took a few years before the war, to spend the festive season with some old friends in the country, I had a succession of curious puzzling experiences. When I set out from home my first perplexity began. The railway station was four miles from my house; I had two heavy bags of equal weight, and my horse had suddenly gone lame. There was no time to hire a conveyance, so it was clear I must walk. But I could not alone manage the two bags. My gardener and the boy both insisted on carrying the luggage, but the gardener was an old man and the boy not sufficiently strong, and, as I believe in a fair division of labour, and in taking my own share, I settled that we should all three walk to the station together and share the burden equally among us. So we started off with the gardener carrying one bag and the boy the other, while I worked out in my head the best way of arranging for the transfer of the bags as we went along. How would you have done it?

THE STATIONMASTER'S REPLY.

When we reached the railway station I asked the stationmaster how long I had to wait for my train, and he answered, "Too-too-too-too-too-too." I overheard the boy say to the gardener, "I should like to punch his head for speaking to the governor like that. Why can't he give a civil answer?" But the answer was quite civil when properly understood. Now, what did the stationmaster mean by his curious trumpeting?

THE MOTOR-CAR FARE.

Well, I broke my journey at Addleford, and hired a motor-car to take me out to Clinkerville, where I had a sick aunt. In passing through the village of Bakenham, just midway between Addleford and Clinkerville, who should I meet but my old friend Watkins? I agreed to take him on to Clinkerville and bring him back to Bakenham on my return journey. Watkins is an eccentric fellow, and he insisted on paying his fair share of the hire. As I paid £3 myself for the car, what was the correct portion of the fare that Watkins should have contributed?

Most people trip up over this very simple little question.

CHRISTMAS-TREE PRESENTS.

When I got to London, where I was breaking the journey for the night, I went round to see my old friend Bradgate. His family were preparing a large Christmas-tree for a number of poor children in their district, and I found they wanted some small toys to complete it. So I went to a shop and bought sixty little articles for five shillings. All the wooden toys cost threepence each, all the toys made of tin cost twopence each, and every packet of sweets cost a halfpenny each. Now, as I bought just five times as many tin toys as wooden, I wonder whether you can tell how many there were of each kind to make up the exact money.

THE FAMILY PARTY.

The Bradgates told me they were having a family gathering for the season. It was to consist of 1 grandfather, 1 grandmother, 2 fathers, 2 mothers, 4 children, 3 grandchildren, 1 brother, 2 sisters, 2 sons, 2 daughters, 1 father-in-law, 1 mother-in-law, and 1 daughter-in-law.

"Quite a large party," I can hear the reader say. "There were 23 persons in all."

No; you are quite wrong. There were only seven persons altogether. Can you tell me how this could have been?

A CHARITABLE DISTRIBUTION.

Finally, next day, while I was walking, a number of men, who seemed to me really deserving of help, appealed to me for assistance. I had a certain amount of loose cash in my pocket (13s. 9d. to be exact), and I said I would divide it equally amongst them. As, in doing this, I found it absolutely necessary to give at least six coins to every man, you will find it a little perplexing to discover from that fact exactly how many men there were to share the gift.

(The answers to the above puzzles will appear in BLIGHTY for Dec. 19.)

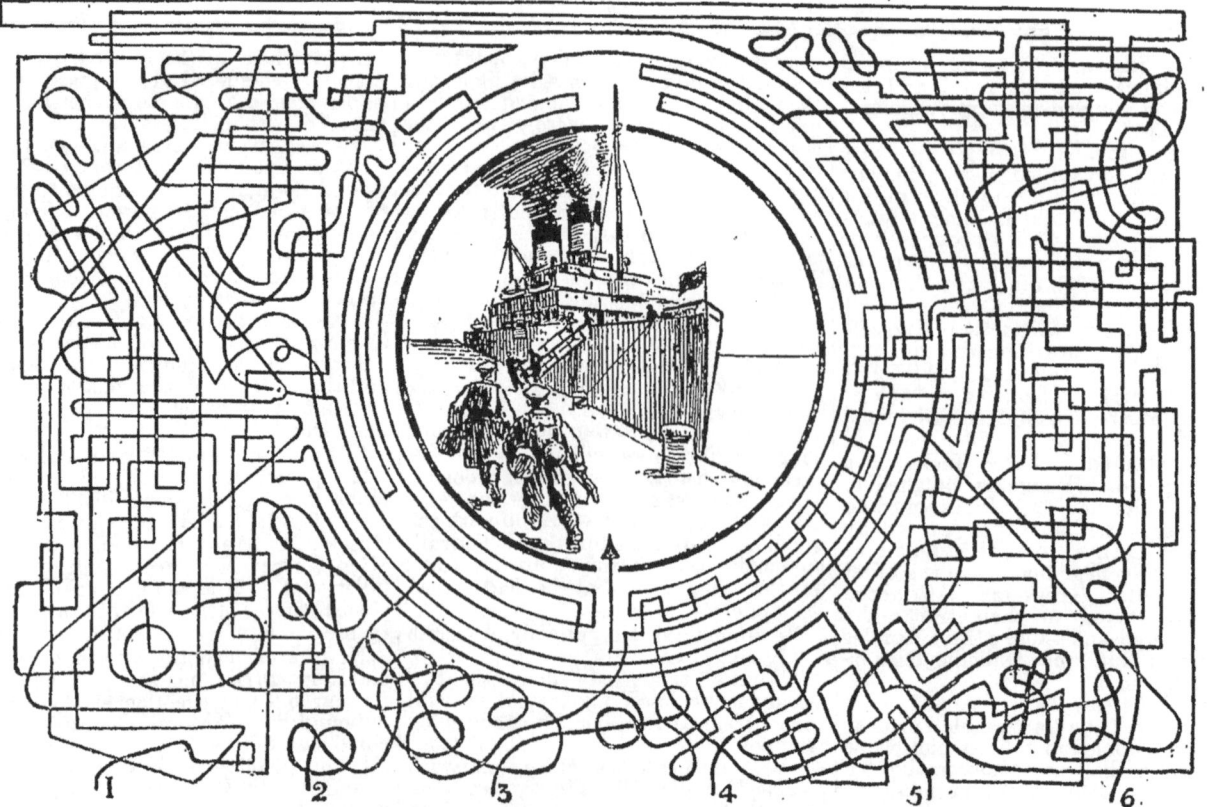

CAN YOU CATCH THE BOAT FOR BLIGHTY?

Instructions: THE PUZZLE IS TO FIND THE LINE THAT LEADS TO THE SHIP IN THE CENTRE, STARTING FROM POINTS 1, 2, 3, 4, 5, OR 6.

Instructor: "PULL UP, PULL UP, SIR—YOU MUSTN'T GALLOP THE HORSE LIKE THAT!"
Dr. Doolan: "ALL ROIGHT, ALL ROIGHT, SERGEANT! OI'M ONLY SHOWING THE BHOYS HOW TO DO AN HOUR'S EXERCISE IN TWINTY MINUTES!"
Cpl. G. H. Warwick, 123 Bde. H.Q.

CONCERNING "BLIGHTY."

This Christmas Number is the work of our sailors and soldiers on active service. In the intervals of "strafing" the Hun they find leisure to write and to draw, and they have produced a Christmas Blighty to amuse the good folks at home, who for many months have sent out the weekly Blighty to amuse them.

Week by week for eighteen months the ordinary issue of Blighty (made up chiefly of reprints from "Punch" and other papers and magazines) has been published for our fighting forces and sent out to them as a free gift, for love and remembrance. These weekly numbers are not shown on the bookstalls or sold to the public; they are sent straight from the printers to the Front and the Fleet, to the Red Cross hospitals and the Y.M.C.A. huts, to the bases and the rest camps and the trenches of the firing line.

The little paper goes to France and Flander, to Egypt and Salonica and Mesopotamia, to India and Africa, to the North Sea and the Mediterranean and the Atlantic patrols—wherever our men are fighting for us. Blighty is their favourite paper—so they tell us in hundreds of letters—because it is their very own paper, published for them and for them alone.

The Christmas Number is different. It is made up of contributions from our readers themselves, and it is sold to the public to provide money for keeping up the weekly publication of Blighty. Last year the Christmas Number produced enough profit to pay the expenses of the ordinary issue for seven weeks.

Few people outside the newspaper business have any idea what it costs to produce even a small weekly periodical, with paper at its present price. Blighty was started in May, 1916, and from that date to the end of June last we received £21,000 in donations and spent £23,000 on producing and sending out the journal.

We are thus in the unique position, for a charity, of devoting to the actual work not only every penny the public subscribed, but a great deal more. Yet we are not in debt. The profits of our Christmas Number and our revenue from advertisements paid the difference, and paid also all the cost of circulars and advertisements appealing for donations. There are no "expenses of administration"; the work of our Committee and of our Secretary, Auditors, and Legal Advisers, is gratuitous.

We have even a bit of money in hand, after sending out over six million copies of Blighty free. But the expenses are continuous, and the price of paper threatens to be heavier than ever in the coming year. So we want every reader of this Christmas Number to send us something towards the New Year, so that the boys may not go short of cheerful reading to brighten their dull days and help to keep them smiling amidst the daily routine of discomfort, danger, and death.

In thanking all those who have so generously helped us in the past we offer a special tribute of respectful gratitude to Her Majesty Queen Alexandra, who has been good enough to take a personal interest in Blighty from its start. Twice she has favoured us with her Royal signature to our "Christmas Greeting," and the following letter evinces her kindly sympathy and appreciation of our efforts.

A ROYAL FAVOUR.

General Sir Dighton Probyn, Controller to H.M. Queen Alexandra, writes us as follows:—

"Your letter for Queen Alexandra, enclosed in your letter to me of the 13th instant, I duly submitted to Her Majesty.

"In reply to the same, I am desired by the Queen to inform you that Her Majesty has great pleasure in complying with your request, and I now enclose one of Her Majesty's autograph signatures to be reproduced with 'Blighty's' Christmas Greeting, which this year, Her Majesty observes, is intended to be from The Women at Home.

"I am further desired by Queen Alexandra—Her Majesty knowing how much 'Blighty' is appreciated by all—to forward for the Committee of 'Blighty' a cheque for £10, as a Christmas donation from Her Majesty towards the Funds of your excellent publication."

"YAH! I CAN GIT BANANAS DAHN THE STREET FOR A PENNY."
"YUS, THEM'S FURRIN ONES—OURS ARE REAL ENGLISH."
H. Mallalieu.

LEAVING MY 'OME IN OSSIE.

Gor blime! 'ow ther days drag on an' on
  Since first I left me little canvas 'ome
    Ter 'stonish Bill Kaiser; strafe ther blarsted ——!

* * * * * *

Do you remember, mum? All Wongan shone
  Beneath ther mornin' sun. Ther choc'late loam
    Of Wongan Hills, new-broken by ther plow,
Smelt strangely sweet, familiar-like, and dear.
The 'orses, they come running to ther rails
  As down among the salmon gums I come.
Ther world were still that mornin', couldn' 'ear
  A single sound excep' the 'orses' tails
    Flickin' ther flies away. I tell yer, mum,
Yer think me mighty brave, I tell yer straight
  I stood there wiv me 'and upon ther door
    Afraid ter make a sound an' wake yer all.
I knew yer must be tired, sleepin' late,
  An' dreamin' ov ther days before the war,
    Perraps, w'en Ern an' Midge an' I was small,
An' all ov us was 'appy. 'Ere was me
  Acomin' 'ome to say me larst farewell
    An 'break yer 'eart an' go. By gum, this war
Comes damned 'ard on ther wimmen. Such as we
  'Oo go an' fight, 'ave only 'arf the 'ell
    Our wommen suffer. Mum, before
I yeiled out "Anyone at 'ome?" that day,
  Me 'eart stood still wiv fear. But w'en yer woke,

Gor blime, mum, I could 'ave 'owled, ther way
That you took on an' mugged this child. An' Fay
  An' little Nance stood by an' never spoke,
    But jus' kep' gazin' up as if ter say
That they was proud of their big bruvver. Mum,
It makes me feel a lump down in me froat

"HELP!—CAN'T STOP THE CAR!—LOST THE BOOK OF INSTRUCTIONS!"
Pte. B. Rutherford,
36th Batt., A.I.F.

When I remember! Then ole dad come in
  An' gripped me by the 'and. Fair dinkum, mum,
    I never knew yer was so fond ov me
Till that larst day before I caught ther boat.
While dad an' I was talkin' ov ther crop
  An' other matters, stole a 'and in mine,
    An' there was Midge beside me large as life.
By gum, if there's one thing I value top
  Ov all things in the 'appy fortune line,
    It's this—to 'ave 'er equal for me wife.
There ain't a better sister saw ther light
  Than dear ole Midge. Well, mum, the day was done
    Too soon for all ov us, an' when at length
Come down on Wongan Hills ther purple night
  That meant I'd 'ave ter say "good-bye." This son
    Ain't fought a fight wiv quarter ov ther strength
As what 'e fought that night. Yer eyes, ole mum,
  Was shinin' like ther stars wiv tears 'eld back.
    Poor Midge was cryin' like 'er 'eart 'd break,
An' Nance and Fay was looking mighty glum.
  Dad couldn' speak, but gave the 'orse a crack.
    The war's a bastard, mum, an' no mistake.

"THE MASTER OF THE FAMILY."

※

Staff-Sergt. (Irish): "Are you smoking here—lying on the bundles of straw?"
"Yes, Staff."
"Why, you'll have the place alight before you have time to put it out."

TEN LITTLE SOLDIER BOYS.

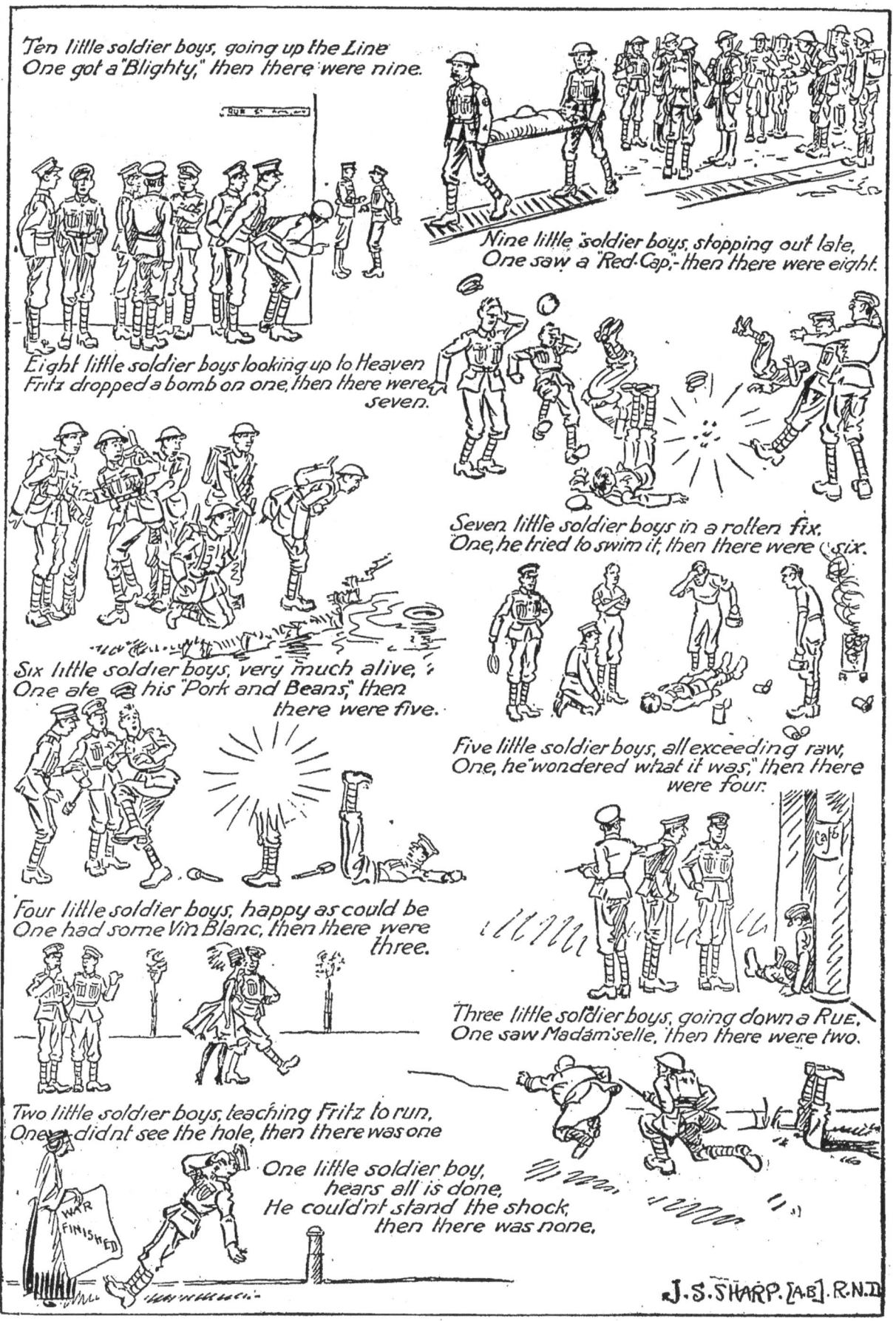

A. B. Sharp, Howe Batt., R.N.D.

THE SCROUNGER.

A Scrounger? Yes, perhaps I am. What then?
Is it a sin to scrounge, to ask a fag,
To beg a woodbine or a piece of soap,
When times are hard, and pay day seems remote?
I trow not, and indeed it seems to me
That this is friendship, this the essential thing,
To share and share alike, sans afterthought,
If you are flush, why then 'tis nothing much
To lend a bob and maybe two, and so
To keep on lending till you're broke, and then
The scrounged-on can turn scrounger, and will find
A friend to help him in the hour of need.
Is it right that Basil Thomson over there
Should get seven bob a week and ten from home,
Whilst I, who have a needy mother, send
Five bob to Poplar weekly, leaving two,
Not much to slake an ever present thirst?
It seems unjust and so, to put it right,
I sometimes meet him in the coffee bar,
And there, with pleasant chat engage him, while
He waits his turn and then, being on the spot,
I ask him how he's fixed and he, the toff,
The pursy boy, the lad, the man of means,
Will stand me cheerfully a cup of tea
With wad or brick, or p'r'aps a plate of figs.
The tea being finished, Basil rises and
Will buy himself a packet of navy cut,
Or maybe gold flake, when I gently hint
That I am also fagless, and the lad
Sticks me a packet too, and finally,
Lends me a bob till pay day, and I go
For richer pleasures to the wet canteen.
And if I always cannot pay the debt
In cash, I'll do him little services;
I'll roll his coat, or help him with his kit,
Or fix his straps, or give him friendly tips,
And so we're quits, or near enough, and when
We're in the trenches, other chaps may find
The scrounger at the end will pay in full.

E. G. HOGAN.

FILLING UP THE SHELL-HOLES.

He wasn't on reserve, he wasn't forced to serve,
  But he's filling up the shell-holes in the road.
He's in a "Veteran Corps," in an atmosphere of war,
  And he's filling up the shell-holes in the road.
His soldier days were over, and a "civvy life" he led,
But at the nation's battle-cry he started seeing "red."
He couldn't get a rifle, so he got a spade instead,
  For filling up the shell-holes in the road.

Once he used to track, with a rifle and a pack;
  Now he's filling up the shell-holes in the road.
He dreams between his pipes of how he earned his stripes
  (But not with filling shell-holes in the road).
Stories he could tell you of a desert so accursed,
Of India, and Egypt, and of men who died of thirst,
Of a little British Army that would always get there
    "First,"
  As he's filling up the shell-holes in the road.

The ribands on his breast are full of interest,
  As he's filling up the shell-holes in the road.
His hair is flecked with grey, he's not so young to-day,
  As he's filling up the shell-holes in the road.
His manner's just as martial, time has lightly with him
    dealt,
He's hardly quite as active, as he was upon the veldt.
He's grown a trifle stouter in the region of the belt,
  As he's filling up the shell-holes in the road.

Of two bonny sons he's proud, and their praise he'll sing
    aloud,
  As he's filling up the shell-holes in the road.
He saw them "on the Somme," in a draft that came along,
  While filling up the shell-holes in the road.
Next morning they went over, in the first attacking wave,
And when they brought the news to him, "They'd fallen
    with the brave,"
He wished he had been with them to have shared a sol-
    dier's grave,
  'Stead of filling up the shell-holes in the road.

Sgt. G. E. ATTWOOD.

'17: "WHICH D'YOU RECKON THE BEST BADGE IN THE ARMY?"
'14: "WELL, I THINK THAT SILVER ONE THEY HAVE AT HOME WANTS SOME BEATING."

S. P. and Pte. H. Wilding, 144 Labour Coy.

LONDON FEMALE GUARDIAN SOCIETY.

Patron—H. M. THE KING.   President—LORD KINNAIRD, K.T.

Courteous Reader! This National Rescue Society sorely needs your help to maintain its large family of young girls. During the past 117 years it has rescued from the streets some thousands of Betrayed and Fallen Girls, some of whom were defenceless victims of the White Slave Traffic, and now in these dark days of War, when the cost of maintenance is alarming, its need is multiplied. Will you, therefore, kindly

COME TO OUR AID

by sending a Christmas Gift, addressed to "The Committee," LONDON FEMALE GUARDIAN SOCIETY, 191, High Street, Stoke Newington, LONDON, N. 16.

Lt.-Col. G. B.——, D.C.O., writes:—
"They must have saved me several pounds in boots."
A BRIGADIER-GENERAL in France, writes:—
"I cannot imagine anyone who has once tried these Soles ever being without them."

Phillips' 'Military' SOLES and HEELS.

¶ Thin rubber plates, with raised studs, to be attached on top of ordinary soles and heels, giving complete protection from wear. The rubber used is **six times more durable** than leather.

¶ They impart smoothness to the tread, give grip, and prevent slipping. Feet kept dry in wet weather.

From all Bootmakers, or ask for them at the Canteens.

Fortify your Boots!

Per Set
MEN'S STOUT (Active Service) 5/6
LADIES' (for Red Cross Workers, etc.) ... 3/-

Phillips' Patents, Ltd. (Dept. S.2) 142-6, Old St., London, E.C.

For the Trenches.

"KAMPITE"
(Patent applied for)

SAFETY TRENCH COOKER

NO SPIRIT   NO LIQUID

CHEAP, CLEAN AND RELIABLE

6½D

Complete with Collapsible stand and Six Fuel Blocks.

OBTAINABLE EVERYWHERE.

Three Boxes sent direct to the Trenches for 2/6 post paid.

BRYANT & MAY, Ltd. (Dept. K 14), BOW, LONDON, E.

END OF THE WAR.

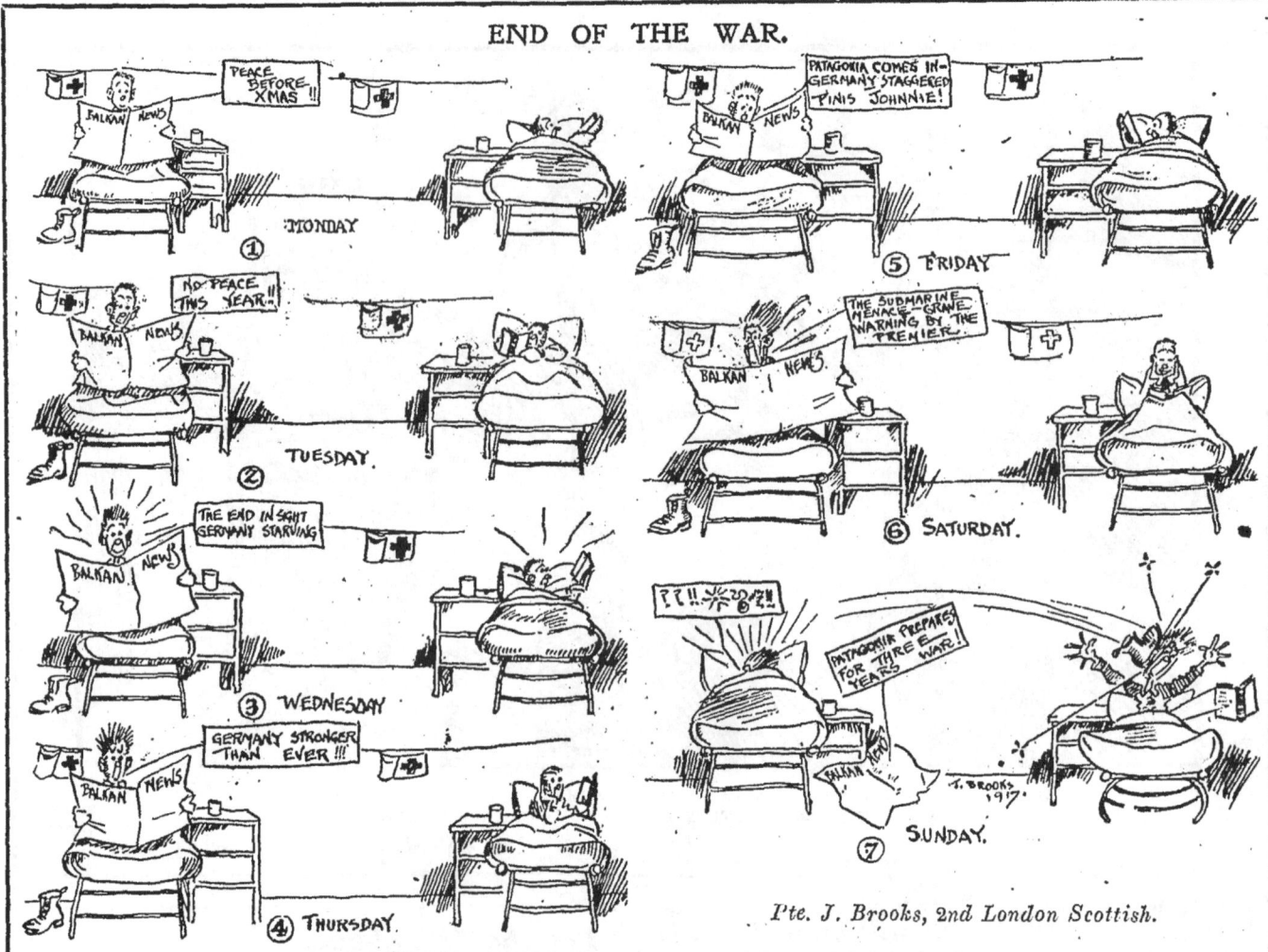

Pte. J. Brooks, 2nd London Scottish.

A TRAGEDY AVERTED

When I first met James he was sitting on a chair in that popular Rouen rendezvous, the Jardin de Solferino, apparently endeavouring to make the acquaintance of a buxom dame of mature appearance who, on a neighbouring seat, was dividing her time between furious spasms of knitting and fruitless attempts to restrain the youthful energies of two children.

"It's no use," said James, after a strenuous five minutes of what I took to be Morse, to the large lady, who, entirely unmoved, was gathering together her knitting and her children, and preparing to depart.

He turned to me for sympathy. "It's the language that does it. Now, if I could parley-voo —— Bon secours, madame," he broke off quickly, as the lady swept by with her progeny. "Ally voo biang cette apri midi. Jer voo——. No, it's not a bit of use," and he mopped his forehead wearily, while the object of his addresses moved out of earshot. "I shall never be a success out here."

"Come, come," I remonstrated encouragingly. "It's not as bad as all that, surely. What exactly is the trouble?"

"She was the fifth this afternoon," he began in a dreamy reminiscent sort of tone. "And they were all peaches. The first one had a blue hat and walked from her hips. You know what I mean, don't you?"

I pretended that I did.

"But, as I say, it wasn't a bit of use," James went on sadly. "I walked alongside her for two paths trying to think of the French for hat, so as to open the conversation in an agreeable manner, and then just as I remembered it, up came one of those A.S.C. blighters and snapped her up under my very nose. And it was just the same with the others. An Australian collared one, a Highlander another, while the third went off with a Belgian. Rotten taste, I call it!"

He was silent for a moment. Then his roving eye encountered an affectionate meeting between a much-moustached sergeant-major and a pretty little bonne scarcely out of her teens.

"Just look at that, now I ask you! At his time of life, too! I'd S.M. him with half a chance! And look all around you," and he waved his hand in a gloomy embrace of the whole garden. "Every blooming regiment in the British Army, and they've all got off, bar me. And it's not looks that does it either," he continued, with his eye still on the sergeant-major. "It's the bally language. Why, if I could speak French I'd have a blinking harem."

"But why don't you learn?" I asked.

"I did go to a French class once," replied James, "but it didn't do me any good. The teacher's idea was to rush round the room, seize various articles of furniture and ask you what the French was for them was. Now, I can't very well go up to a girl, grab her by the leg and say 'Kess ker say ker sa,' can I?"

I admitted that the procedure was scarcely likely to commend itself to the lady concerned.

"Well, there you are then. What's a fellow to do? But if some of these French maddemazelles only knew what they were missing in not going out with me, why——"

What exactly would happen I never knew, for just then an indiarubber ball hit James violently in the face and cut off further speech.

"You Ingleesh soger, you play me?" and a little mite of some five summers stood invitingly before the astonished James.

"Well, I'm jiggered!" he at length managed to gasp. "Why, you're the only one of the whole lot with any sense at all. Play with you? Why, sure!"

When I left the garden half-an-hour later, James was still playing, and, judging from the noise he was making, he had evidently got off to his satisfaction at last.—W. D. MAYDUKE.

Printed by WALBROOK & CO., LTD., Fleet Printing Works, 13-15, Whitefriars Street, E.C. 4, and published by "THE COMMITTEE OF BLIGHTY," at 40, Fleet Street, London, E.C. 4.